UNDER THE CRUCIAN SUN

a memoir of place

WRITTEN & PHOTOGRAPHED

BY

CYNTHIA MCVAY

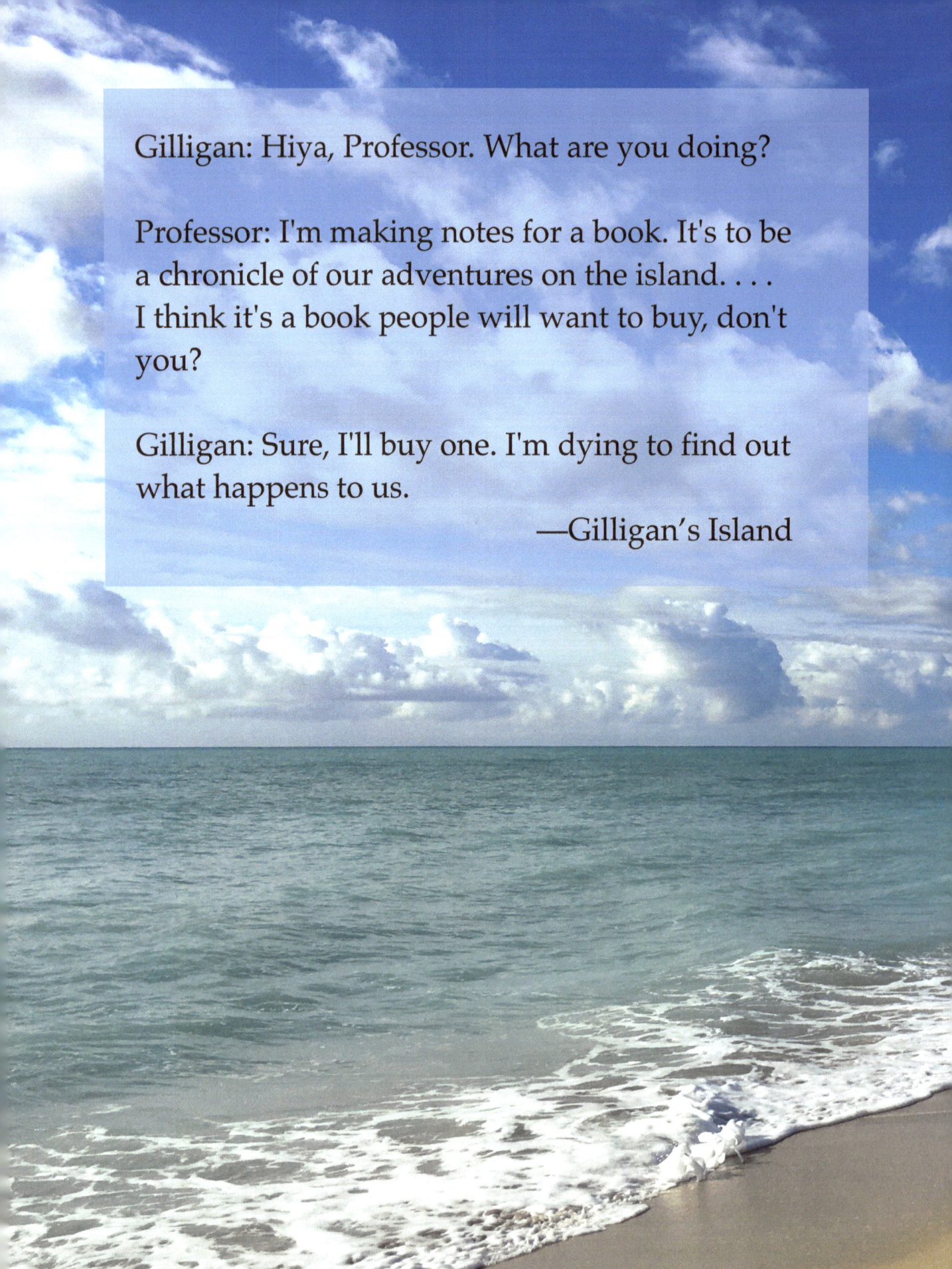

Gilligan: Hiya, Professor. What are you doing?

Professor: I'm making notes for a book. It's to be a chronicle of our adventures on the island. . . . I think it's a book people will want to buy, don't you?

Gilligan: Sure, I'll buy one. I'm dying to find out what happens to us.

—Gilligan's Island

CONTENTS

MY ISLAND HOME   6

WHY ST CROIX?   10
ARRIVING   17
ONE PEARL   23
FLAMBOYANT HILL   34
THE RESURRECTION   48
THE RUSTY TANK   62
BEES AND BATTERIES   69

LIVING IN A PLACE   76

FRESH IMPRESSIONS   78
EMBRACING INVASIVES   83
NEIGHBORHOOD LAUNDRY   87
PRINTOUT   90
A BREEZY AFFAIR   95
HOUSES OF ST. CROIX   97
IN LINE AT WAPA   103

DANCE! 110
ADULT PARADE 116
WINDING DOWN 124

SKY, WATER, SAND 126

BLUE AND BLUE AND BLUE 128
PELICAN COVE 131
HA' PENNY 143
BEACH MATH/RULES 158
THE FREDERIKSTED PIER 160
POLYSANDORY 167
INDEX OF LIFE ON ST CROIX 178

ACKNOWLEDGEMENTS 197

APPRECIATION 197
PREVIOUSLY PUBLISHED 197

"I take up my pen just to give you an imperfect account"

—Alexander Hamilton, to *The Royal Danish American Gazette*, 6 September 1772

WHY ST CROIX?

I am drawn—no, I am addicted— to saving wrecks and ruins. I tried to quit, but I can't help myself. They beckon. I get my fix from fixing them, putting them back together. I've always been this way, I suppose, by nature a problem solver, and self-appointed savior of interesting architecture, good design and historic buildings. I wish I could fall for a turnkey, finished home like normal people, but they hold little attraction. For me, there's no challenge or mystery or story. I love older structures for their understated elegance, placement in the land, mature vegetation, use of organic materials, unabashed mark of activity and time, and their (often) simple, timeless even modern lines driven by function. Their layouts, priorities and proportions make sense to me. I don't need a walk-in closet, or a kitchen the size of a gymnasium or a media room. I minimally renovate, just enough for basic creature comforts, in part because I am a frugal environmentalist, but mostly out of respect for the original intentions of the makers. Urgency accompanies older buildings, too. I worry that they will crumble beyond recognition, or—worse—someone else will "renovate" and ruin them, "gut" them, which to many signifies improvement, but generally involves removing character: uneven floorboards, old glass, plaster walls. I don't restore in a period kind of way; I have no desire to live in the past. My mission is to reveal their souls.

That's how I arrived on St. Croix, ready to save a property in the middle of a dog-day summer, the result of minimal research and a series of incremental decisions which made perfect sense every step of the way. Friends are likely polite and humoring me, but they ask, *Why St. Croix?* It's a valid question. On the island, *Why St. Croix?* is a conversation starter. Everyone has a story about how they ended up here, many reasonable: they visited as a child; they wanted to retire with good climate and certain amenities; they came to work with FEMA after a hurricane and never left; they are taking advantage of tax breaks; or they came to participate in the triathlon and fell in love. None of those apply to me. Let's back up.

In 2017, I sold a mammoth 1840s stone house on seven acres in New York's Hudson Valley, with six outbuildings including a chicken coop, enormous barn and stone smokehouse, which I'd bought as an investment in 2010. I was letting it go because—at a half hour from where I lived—it was too far and too much work. I had brought it back from the brink, tried to find a tenant, but no one could afford to rent a house that had been four separate apartments with seven bedrooms. I Airbnbed it for a few years, but soon tired of spending two half days every week preparing for and cleaning up after a dozen Airbnb guests who came in all kinds of unruly permutations. When I sold it for a modest profit, my real estate lawyer suggested doing a 1031 Exchange, which allows a seller to reinvest the funds into a like investment to postpone paying capital gains taxes. I was trying to simplify my life, so I was not interested in taking on another property. But with her encouragement, I placed the proceeds of the sale of the house into escrow, just in case something came along.

The 1031 Exchange has non-negotiable deadlines and rules, such as needing to identify the new property within 45 days of selling the original property and closing on the new one within 180 days. And it only applies in the U.S. So, while Mexico, my old stomping grounds, would be a natural wintering and retirement destination for me, where the adobe architecture is appealing, food is crunchy, comforting and healthy, beaches are hands down among the best in the world—I thought, until I came to St. Croix—Mexico was not an option. Neither was the 11-bedroom, 13th-century villa-ruin in Tuscan-nowhere with frescoes and wide beams, high-vaulted ceilings and a vista to boot that I had been "visiting" online for half a year.

I was dating a guy we'll call Pete, eight years my senior, who was separated but not divorced. His not-quite-ex had not allowed him to pursue his dream of having a place in the sun. While Pete was kind, an artist, generally willing and somewhat able, he was also quirky, compulsive, smothering and high maintenance. In a word, exhausting. I wasn't sure about us and our future. Nonetheless, he wanted a real estate project, and he seemed like an appropriate person with whom to embark on an adventure. But it was hard to separate the

project from this man about whom I had significant reservations. And a piece of me felt that Pete saw this project as relationship security.

I thought about places where I wanted to spend time, which would also be a warm escape during the increasingly hostile, barren and unpredictable New York winters. Even with all the Hudson Valley has to offer 85 miles north of New York City, January and February can be bleak; days are short, many cultural venues shutter. I had to balance owning a second home with how it would limit other travel, and how to accommodate my run-like-the-wind English Setter Dexter. I started scrolling through Zillow listings, broadly, all over the country, and fantasized about where I could live. We took a road trip to Martha's Vineyard and saw a couple dozen properties in two days—lacy Sears-Roebuck Victorians, suburban homes with perfect grass and asphalt driveways, asbestos-laden foreclosures and beach shacks. I considered expanses of land in the west, Frank Lloyd Wright houses, Eichler mid-centuries in the Bay Area and historic homes in Savannah. A couple caught my eye, but owning an interesting home in a random place, where I knew no one, made little sense.

All were much further away than a half hour and would not simplify my life, but make life much more complicated, of course.

How about Puerto Rico? I could invest, albeit modestly, in the hurricane-thrashed economy. A sort of a watered-down Latin America, Puerto Rico had recently been through hurricane hell. I could get a good deal, while helping to rebuild. But—can you imagine?—1031 Exchanges do not apply to Puerto Rico. The US Virgin Islands do qualify, however, as an unincorporated territory.

I'd never been to the USVI. In fact, a decade before, I'm not sure I knew St. Croix existed. My parents and sister had spent a holiday week on St. John a year I couldn't join them. It looked lovely, essentially a National Park, was precious, expensive and hard to get to—a flight to St. Thomas, then a ferry. Probably a better place to visit than to live. My daughter Tess had been to St. Thomas with a friend. The governing center of the USVI, St. Thomas was difficult to pinpoint from a lifestyle or texture point of view but seemed to revolve around cruises, duty-free shopping and partying. St. Croix was for living and was making an agricultural play. A couple of interesting towns had European names: Christiansted and Frederiksted. I zeroed in on St. Croix. With a population of roughly 50,000 at that time (the latest census in 2020 showed it dropped to 40,000 after the refinery closed) and about 28 miles from end to end.

I scoured every offering on Zillow; it seemed like the entire island was for sale. Many of the houses in my price range were small concrete boxes, all with the same glazed white tile and tired furniture, and they were unfortunately being sold *furnished*. Was it because living on an island afforded few decorating choices? Irma and Maria had rolled through a year earlier so about a tenth of the listings were hurricane-damaged, and sold AS IS. Some of these interested me more, offering the opportunity to purchase at a discount, then finish and furnish to my liking. But these properties also served as warnings: if a house was hit by a hurricane once, was it more likely to be hit again? What do the laws of probability and physics say about that?

I saved dozens of listings and clicked "CONTACT AGENT" on a couple.

I heard back from Alice. She said she was not really the agent for the property, and the place didn't really exist, but she could help me.

By then I'd seen crumbling stone structures in the yards of a couple listings. What were those? While I hadn't been to St. Croix, I had traveled to other islands in the Caribbean. On Nevis and in Curaçao, I had stumbled across old plantations, some renovated into inns. I wondered if St. Croix had similar historic structures.

I told Alice I wanted something with architectural features as an investment. She translated "investment" to "commercial," which didn't interest me at all. Finally, in a triad of listings, one caught my eye. It was vacant and unfurnished. In fact, it was abandoned, possibly for decades: 1 Pearl in Kingshill in Queen's Quarter. I liked the ring to the address. A flat nine acres 150 feet above sea level, it sat back from the road. In one of the dozens of photos, a stone read *1657*. The drone video showed outdoor walkways framing arches on two sides of a courtyard with a maze of shorn hedges. The stone walls were three feet thick. A Tuscan villa in the Caribbean, where it was warm (hot? horrendously hot?) year round! Peeling plaster. Old lamps. Brightly-hued rooms in older photos, with deep, Corbusier-like recessed window openings. Wooden shutters hung from a single hinge or were missing. It was a mess. It was perfect. I was in love.

I read documents, posted and buried in the listing information. A previous resident sent an email fifteen years earlier inquiring about 1 Pearl's history. I Googled the owners' names. He had died ten years

before; she died a few years later. The obituaries described how involved each was in the island's culture and environmental initiatives. They sounded wonderful. I wanted to be them. As far as I was concerned, they were handing me the baton. Scanned mimeographs of longhand script from yesteryear documented the history of the estate, beginning with the Knights of Malta, including accounting of enslaved and free peoples, which may or may not be specific to the property. Alice wrote, "This is one the oldest buildings in all of the Caribbean." I believed her.

In the 1700s there were roughly 2,000 Europeans on St. Croix, and ten times as many enslaved. It baffles me that the Europeans weren't overthrown, although there was a squelched uprising after emancipation, an ugly reminder of the Dane's brutality.

Further, I was learning that Hamilton grew up on St. Croix. The hit musical was workshopped at Powerhouse Theater while resident at Vassar College in 2013 twenty minutes from my home in the Hudson Valley. Funny that I might end up wintering on a tiny island in the Caribbean where the story originated.

I was in constant correspondence with Alice. I woke with her. I went to bed with her. She kept sending me other listings, other historic buildings, mostly commercial, in town, with "good tenants," like a night club or a boutique. I wasn't interested in being a landlord, but she heard "investment." She sent me plots overlooking beaches. None drew me in like 1 Pearl in Kingshill.

My 45 days were almost up for the 1031 Exchange. I submitted my short list, including a couple empty plots and "my" "Pearl."

But wait. I'd never been to St. Croix. It was far away. Certainly, further than the house I just sold. Not 22 minutes, but 7 hours by plane, and a stop.

We booked our flights.

ARRIVING

We arrived at 10:00 PM, mid-August 2018, at the Henry E. Rohlsen Airport in pouring rain. Pete went to the Hertz window while I retrieved our gate-checked carry-on bag. I scrolled through my phone for the directions to our Airbnb. The on-property manager, Ty, had said that Google maps knew it as "Discovery Grove." We exited the airport, following the lights of the cars ahead of us. Driving on the left side of the road—with the steering wheel on the left— would take some getting used to.

One by one, the other cars peeled away, and the island was enveloped in darkness. We no longer had taillights to follow to remind us where to be and couldn't see much beyond the beam of our headlights. A military base. Flat land. Austere fences. The road dipped frequently and made some big ninety-degree bends. We turned left onto our final road, passed over a small bridge and ascended into a tropical rainforest. Peepers and crickets filled the night. Dense foliage, vines, and trunks angled over the road. We slowed, looking for a stone column, as directed. *Discovery Grove*, and a handwritten sign beneath: *1B*. We careened downward into the night, following gravel rivulets over a small bridge, with a casual chain and no railing. Dogs barked. A light was our beacon a few hundred feet in.

Our headlights caught a tall man ducking through the doorway of a small house, waving his long limbs to continue up the driveway. He shouted at the three excited canines who we'd been warned about in the Airbnb listing, a warning we'd ignored, uneducated about *island dogs*. The tires of our small rental car spun on the wet stones on the incline. I had been excited to find the sugar mill on Airbnb: a round, stone emblem connected to St. Croix's plantation history.

Ty's energy exceeded what was required for the time of night. Gangly, in long shorts, his enthusiasm for the island filled the room. He stood with his legs separated several feet, beyond his own shoulder width, the angle of his legs echoing the sugar mill's walls. The same long arms that waved at the dogs were pointing at the bathroom up the stairs, and the other direction, where to shower, back out the door, down a long flight of stairs, behind a communal kitchen, shared with other guests.

"You should use the toilet in your own room, you know, just in case. . . . " he said, smiling.

He'd arrived from Idaho ten years before.

"Who owns this place?" I asked.

"It was sold a couple days ago. The owner never came down anymore, so she put it on the market." Four buildings, thirteen acres, and a mill turned into a suite. I was sorry to have missed the opportunity, but it was likely beyond my budget.

Although our round ample, sugar mill had a bed on the first floor, Ty encouraged us

to sleep upstairs, where mosquito netting draped over the bed, while insisting mosquitoes weren't a problem. The circular staircase was precarious, ascending from normal to irregular spacing at a seventy-degree angle. The railing, too, wouldn't offer much support if called upon in an emergency, like when you were falling, like when you needed it. Two thirds of the way up the stairs, a half bath—something of a cantilevered shrine holding a toilet and sink the size of clasped hands—jutted out onto a landing built of louvre windows. A folding door opened to provide visual but not audio privacy. From below, the bathroom sat at an odd angle, from the second floor, getting into the bathroom was like jumping over a ravine—the ravine being the stairwell. If you were a sleepwalker or a drinker, this bathroom could separate you from those who weren't, and life, possibly forever.

    I cranked open all the louvre windows with screening. We slept with our heads at the foot of the bed under the fan which we ran at high speed. Ty was right: there were no mosquitoes, just a riot of external nightlife: crickets, tree frogs, *coquis*. The sultry night cooled enough to provide a restless sleep, restless more from excitement and newness than anything else. The mill was a perfect start to our adventure.

    Here we were on St. Croix, after all the buildup, researching, reading, sifting through Zillow updates. I was eager to see 1 Pearl. We were meeting the realtor at 9:00 am, not early enough.

    In the morning, as early risers, we had time to kill. We headed into Christiansted in search of the critical morning jolt of caffeine. We stumbled across Twin City Coffeehouse, seemingly, at that time, the only game in town.

    Three women were busy behind the counter. Pete ordered oatmeal and a cinnamon bun. "Made it myself this morning," one woman said. I pointed at a twisted cheese stick.

    "Go outside. We'll bring it to you." We were taking up too much room, asking too many questions.

    A petite young woman delivered our lattes a few minutes later. When she heard we were from the U.S., she told us that she had received a full scholarship to attend college on the continent, to study biology, premed. She was numbers-nimble and dutiful, and diffident. I was excited for her, but wondered how she would make out on a campus the size of the entire island.

    I would build a future life around those lattes, and get to know Theresa and Izler, the power duo not only behind the cafe, but 340 Women's Soccer Club.

    An older man, with rugged features, sat on the corner of the patio, with *Avis*, the local newspaper. He and his wife arrived forty years earlier to teach, and fell in love with the island.

    "How'd you fare during Hurricane Maria?"

    "We were without power for 180 days."

    "But you decided to stay."

"Yes." He paused. "When you're older, you have fewer options."

"We're thinking about buying a place down here," I said, possibly with too much enthusiasm.

He turned to me. "I would just say, take your time. Get to know the island."

Pete and I looked at one another. Ha! I arrived committed to a specific property, on a tight timeline, constrained by 1031 Exchange rules.

"Probably a good idea," I said. "See you tomorrow?"

"I'll be here," he said.

I saw the teacher that first year frequently but haven't seen him since.

We talked to everyone we met, to find out how much they loved living on the island, how to transport dogs, anything about 1 Pearl and its mysterious owner and past. Everyone seemed to know everyone, but no one knew the property's seller, Egbert Hall; a search online led me to a campus center at Ithaca College.

We headed to the end of the street, towards the water, where Fort Christiansvaern stretched along the waterfront, aglow in the morning sun. The grass was dry and short. We bent into a doorway, that shouted, *DUCK!* A tidy, uniformed national park guard sold us tickets. We headed into the fort, symmetrically built around a courtyard, weathered, yellow, sturdy. The canon balls were stacked and soldered together, presumably so they wouldn't become souvenirs. Below, dungeons and small spaces once confined, one with a ceiling

so low the imprisoned could not stand. Alexander Hamilton's mother Rachel Faucette was imprisoned here by her first husband for adultery and flirtatious behavior. Lisa Cantrell, who grew up on St. Croix, said they were still jailing people there during her childhood.

After exploring the possibility of a visit to Buck Island and snorkeling the reefs later in the week, we headed to Alice's office. I'd exchanged hundreds of emails and texts with Alice, her wide grin and beach hair photo beside each. Here she was.

"When is the inspector coming?" she asked.

"At ten tomorrow, Wednesday. Did you line up the contractors for Thursday?" I'd asked Alice to line up contractors to meet us at the property—we'd exchanged a dozen emails on the topic— since time was scarce and of essence, and the tradesmen would know more than any single inspector. They could give a full rundown on what needed to be done, prepare a proposal, so that when we closed on the property—which was inevitable and soon— we could start work immediately. She resisted. I thought if I asked for a list, that would convey how much it meant to me.

"No. You can do that today."

"I'd hoped to have that squared away before I came down." I didn't want to spend precious time on my first day on the island making phone calls.

"You have to be patient down here. Things work at their own pace in St. Croix," she said. I understand cultures have different rhythms. I spent lots of time in Latin America. That is precisely why I wanted to get ahead of it, schedule an electrician, plumber, pool guy, solar installer, to be there, assuming some would be late, others wouldn't show.

"I have a packet of materials for you," she said.

She handed me a laminated folder of her agency with pockets on either side containing the single MLS listing page which I had read hundreds of times and knew by heart.

Later, she gave me a four-page excel printout of what looked like every contractor on the island, not a prioritized shortlist. It was like getting the yellow pages. Maybe realtors aren't allowed to have favorites.

"It isn't up-to-date," she said. She crossed out one name and wrote *DIED*. "Some of the phone numbers may not work."

She wanted me to sign the Offer To Purchase, with their signed counteroffer. We had wanted a signed OTP before we came down, to ensure our trip was not in vain, but there was no reason to initial things now. We were here. I'd stipulated three weeks to do an official and personal inspection, but we'd know in a couple days whether we would we would move forward.

Pete and I followed Alice in our rental car to 1 Pearl heading south, veering to the left, which I learned later was the by-pass. Minutes later, an imposing eight-foot chain-link fence rose up on the right. The listing had said the property was bordered on two sides by fence. This one dipped, laden with pink-flowered vines. I wondered whether this was our fence.

Alice's right blinker flashed. She turned in between two stone columns on either side of the driveway I recognized from the photos. We followed.

ONE PEARL

There was just enough room to pull in behind Alice and off the road. Alice got out of her car and worked the padlock on the gate. We followed her down a dried grass driveway, lined on either side by tall hedges, hints of leaves. Summer's open mouth was parched. A couple hundred feet in, around a gracious curve, we parked under a large tree.

"That's a tamarind. You're lucky," Alice said as we got out.

I looked over at the house, elevated five feet off the ground. I had been here before in my mind. I scoured the photographs, and the drone video, walked around this small, elegant "grand house" so many times, but pieces had been missing. In an instant, it came together.

After three weeks of back and forths, Alice convincing me *this is the one*, it turned out Alice had never set foot on the property, but "sold" it to me sight-unseen, based on the listing. Never mind. 1 Pearl was everything I expected. More. Was this ancient design, or the hand of a previous, more recent owner? At 2,200 square feet, the house was not large, but it was spacious and efficient. The square footage likely did not include the extensive outdoor space: patios and an L-shaped exterior hallway which defined a courtyard in its elbow. Two bathrooms connected three bedrooms without internal hallways. I furnished the rooms in my mind as I walked through providing dimension. *That's where the bed would be, a fan overhead.* Each bedroom had three to four windows, with white shutters hanging on rusting straps and hinges on the outside. There was no glass, no screens. They would need repair, stripping, repainting. Should they remain white or would dare I to go out on a color limb?

The kitchen was, as we knew from the photos, a disaster. Telltale signs of rodent invasion in the ceiling, brown and seeping with excrement, mouse (and we learned later, bat) feces spilled onto the kitchen counters and cabinets. The appliances were ripped out long before, other than the rusty dishwasher, which for some reason I unfortunately opened.

The square kitchen had a window over the stove and another above the sink. A door led to an intimate south-facing patio, from which stairs descended in both directions to another large tamarind tree on one side and—Alice said—a miracle neem on the other. The shade offered a gentle place to take a morning coffee or an afternoon tea. Pressed into the wall, a small stone commemorated the death of someone named Sarah in the early 1800s.

On the other side, the kitchen door swung into an ample dining room. Although spacious with three access doors and various windows, I couldn't imagine when and why anyone would eat inside, on this island that was always eighty degrees and sunny. A large linen closet contained a bag of crisp white tee shirts with animal images, not yet discovered by vermin, which felt out of place, needed an explanation. The ceiling was open; we could see the roof construction which presumably carried throughout the house. The rafters seemed a few decades old, in good condition, but nothing special. I would reseal the ceilings after removing their inhabitants.

A man named Lee Platt purchased and restored the ruin in the 1960s. I found Platt's name connected to the St. Croix Landmark Society, as well as tennis and golf memorials. Lisa Cantrell (a Crucian and a neighbor in the Hudson Valley) told me later that Lee made shadow boxes of military scenes and figures which he sold in his store, Island Imports. He drove a dark green convertible Jaguar. Although sheer speculation, I credit Lee with re-pointing the stone, fortifying the concrete floors and interior walls, building a new roof, and maybe again later, since the current roof and underlying beams didn't seem sixty years old. Perhaps it was rebuilt after Hurricane Hugo in 1989, which destroyed 85% of the homes and businesses on the island. Or maybe that's when the place was left for the second time. No one had any information; I could only imagine.

Other previous occupants were termites: black-brown sandy trails ran up and crisscrossed the yellow wall. They zagged to outlets and switches. They were beautiful in their own way, emoting at once randomness and determination. I was likely the only homeowner to think so.

"Why are they in here? This place is made of stone and concrete," I asked.

Alice said, "Termites eat concrete."

Pete and I looked at one another. To be clear, termites don't eat concrete. Maybe they were reaching for the stars—and the wood in the attic. The trails were dry, no longer active; their presence was menacing and concerning, despite their artistry.

We came across a two-foot square door in the floor, and a loose bundle of twigs nearby.

"That's a rat's nest," Alice said.

"Rats make nests? Like that?" Pete asked with a smile.

He opened the trapdoor. In the cistern's clear water, there was a tangle of filaments, possibly roots. The water could be decades old. Of course, water is as old as time, just recycled. But how long had this particular water sat there? Even if the cisterns held water, we had no assurance that there would be future, fresh water. We discovered concrete gutters on the 70-foot-long bedroom wing which fed the two cisterns. We were learning that well water on the island is brackish. Some potable water comes from a desalination plant. In town, water is piped in. But most residents have cisterns, fed by rainwater caught on their roofs.

Just west of the kitchen and dining room outside was a relic of a wall with old columns and a dry stone fountain. I imagined leaving it much the way it was but cleaning

the 8- by 30-foot space of debris and encouraging certain trees, like the pioneering papaya, and pulling others. Holes in the stone wall likely once hoisted crossbeams, to create an awning or greenhouse or another room. Maybe it would be a shaded arbor. Beyond, I envisioned an in-ground pool, the size of the one back home, 20' X 40', possibly narrower. Not a lap pool, but something with intriguing dimensions. Surrounding, a stone patio would step, along with a grove of fruit trees—lemon, papaya, mango, avocado, coconut palms, or those ones with the red nuts which I learned later are called Christmas palms.

When I visited colleges in California with my daughter Tess ten years before, she asked, "Why doesn't everyone want to live in California?" Valid question! The semi-arid landscape was fascinating and intriguing. If Tess had chosen to go to school there, I would have followed her. That didn't happen, although she moved to San Francisco later (after I committed to St. Croix) and loves it. St Croix offers similar desert and tropical habitat, an antidote to the Hudson Valley's explosive temperate greenness, and dull winters.

Along the long exterior, butchered by electric wires and plumbing, a stone wall created an elevated terrace. After consolidating and burying the mechanicals, we would plant oversized blue-green agave. The maze of walls and clipped hedges at the front of the house, like everything, needed attention. A worn sundial, atop a crumbling brick pillar, told perfect time. This would be another garden, more formal, a respite from the sun, to meander, but also to view from the elevated patio on two sides. A small, dry, round pool would have both water and light and maybe life again.

Across a breezeway from the dining room, through a door graced by a *fleur-de-lis*, and through another door with stones of four awkwardly-proportioned crosses above another, a separate building hosted an ample living room, with five doors. Two opened to a large, roofed patio, atop a double garage. Before I saw it in person, I thought I would screen the large western-facing patio. But with few mosquitoes, even at the height of summer, it no longer seemed necessary. Two arched alcoves on either side begged for statues or candles, and buried into one of the columns was a religious stone carving depicting a prophet and a woman holding a book.

"Uh-oh," Pete said from the edge of the patio.

"What?" I looked over.

It hit me like a ton of bricks. While I was examining sculptures and corners, I had not looked out and up. The western view was occupied by the sleeping refinery, an enormous scar on the horizon: a city of squat and colossal white tanks, banded and striped towers, pipes and tubes feeding stubby and tall stacks and ribbed and girdled cylinders. Empty ladders climbed; exhausts and periscopes poked toward the sky. In- and outlets, horizontal and vertical tubing, inanimate pipelines and ducts at one time transmitted, conveyed, channeled, condensed, syphoned, fused, stirred, whirled. It's a wonder in that maze that all those pipes flowed the right way and did the right thing. Maybe they didn't.

No amount of vegetation could block the twisted metal city, and if it were possible, it would also cloak the open sky and sunset. My heart sunk. Nothing could distract us from the most overwhelming aspect of this view, this room, and the property.

We must have known in that moment that we would not go forward with the purchase, but we were already deeply emotionally and intellectually invested. We continued to explore, on autopilot, trying to forget the overwhelming presence of the refinery, living for as long as we could in our fantasy.

Pete and I had both renovated substantial properties before. We both could imagine in three dimensions, were both handy—he more than I. I knew what needed to be done and had managed electricians, plumbers and other workers in the past on other projects. We worked on our respective Hudson Valley properties and in our gardens, not afraid to be physical or get our hands dirty. Pete's optimism was contagious, and misleading. To him, everything was fixable, doable—buried oil tanks, asbestos, lead paint. And yet when I thought about it, everything he had touched he'd torn down and built from scratch. In that way, he differed—dramatically—from me. I tried to save everything, work with what was given. Restore. Respect. Honor.

But there was nothing he could do about the refinery. There was no way to fix that.

*   *   *

We ventured outside, below the patio where there was a two-car garage with an abandoned kitchen cabinet set. A door off to the side led into a crawl space under the house. A trench, about three feet wide, snaked away into the dark.

"Whoa. Why? What is this for?" I was curious to know where it led, but didn't feel comfortable exploring in the dark.

Alice said, "Lee Platt made it."

"Why?"

"In a craze." We turned away, not satisfied with the answer. I'd ask the building inspector tomorrow.

We decided to get a feel for the property. We bushwhacked through the scrubby forest of thin trees to check out the encroachment on the southwest border I'd noted on the survey. "Ow!" Pete reached for the back of his calf as we walked in the brush.

"What?"

"Something got me." Maybe one of the sand wasps, or Jack Spaniards, Alice warned us about. A huge, black, juicy millipede curled on a tree trunk overhead, and many smaller ones underfoot kept us on our toes. Why was I wearing a cotton dress and sandals? Everything was brittle and thorny, and scratched. This was not a beautiful desert. It was not scrub forest. We came to learn we were in a dense stand of the invasive, non-native tan-tan, also known as false tamarind, found all over the island. Close to impossible to exterminate with their long tap roots and bountiful pods, they can grow twelve feet a year. Maybe a fence would not be necessary on these two sides around the parcel for security and for my dog. The tan-tan was barricade enough for humans and possibly even Dexter.

The encroachment we'd seen on the survey came to life as a clearing and a neighbor's dumping ground: broken tiles, metal rods, garbage, a rusting car. There was a residential neighborhood beyond, with a large construction site underway, in the form of rubble, a church's foundation. It was not clear whether it was a future Church or the remnants of one. But Church-going neighbors seemed like a nice idea.

*   *   *

After two hours of exploring every nook and cranny, we decided to get to know the island, even if 1 Pearl was a no-go. We drove south to the coast in search of the closest beach. Alice told us to look for the twin pink columns of Ha' Penny. We never saw them, which I find amusing in retrospect because they are so obvious, as she said.

We took the southern route east. We were the only ones on the road, other than the mongooses, driving by lovely properties with mills on hills, distant sky-toned villas, goat farms and open arid landscape. We looped back crossing the island, and found a tiny beach where we dipped our feet before a dog discouraged us from further exploration. We returned to Christiansted, parched and hungry. I scanned the guidebook for suggestions. We made our way to Café Christine, located at the back of a shaded, interior courtyard, home to an enormous, landmark mahogany. We drank three quarts of iced red hibiscus tea and shared a chicken sandwich and salad.

Our waitress was the daughter of the cafe's owner, grew up on St Croix and was a student at New York University. As New Yorkers, we marveled at our small world.

A couple women at a neighboring table were friendly. Everywhere, everyone was a font of information. One knew Alice, considered her a friend. She also mentioned that they had opened a dog kennel at 1 Pearl confirming what I'd read. Hence the tee-shirts in the dining room closet.

"Wasn't that the place that guy was killed?" one woman asked, turning to another.

"Someone was killed?" I asked.

"An artist was living there—renting—and her son was shot." Pete and I exchanged glances.

We met our inspector at 10:00 AM the following day. I'm not sure why we decided to follow through with the inspection, when we were no longer going forward with the property, maybe because we'd committed. But I had questions, and always learn something.

Amiable, the inspector told us little we didn't already know. I asked him about the deep trench in the basement and he gamely disappeared into the darkness, lighting his way with his phone into the bowels of the house. I ran to the other side and shouted down a couple of basement windows.

"Hello!!"

He said he could see a little light, but he couldn't hear me. That's how thick the stone walls were. He had no explanation for the tunnel. With all the hurricanes and battles over the years, perhaps this was a bunker from weather or new conquerors.

Above us, Pete measured each room with our new tape measure. I had asked him to pace it out, not caring about exactitude, especially now. But he was obsessive and came away with a scrawl of detailed drawings and numbers to the eighth inch. He said he would use the aerial photo as an outline and reenter the measurements more legibly. At this point, I wondered, why bother?

The inspector brought a generator to test the electrical system, but decided it was unsafe to do so since the meter was ripped out and lay on the garage floor. Many of the outlets were teeming with termite nests. Nonetheless, in his report, he stated that electric was in "fair" or "good" condition. Outlets should be replaced, he said, but we could count on the wires between. We met with an electrician the following day who said that everything would need to be replaced at $250 per point, including all wiring, which amounted to tens of thousands of dollars. The electrical was not in "fair" condition. It was nonexistent. We'd be starting from scratch.

The inspector told us the pile of twigs by the cistern was a thrush nest—not a rat's. He spotted a second two-foot square door in the neighboring bedroom leading to a second cistern, which shared a wall and a pipe to self-regulate water levels. He showed us the overflows that led outside against the house into the bushes, so the cistern wouldn't overfill and explode. Both cisterns needed to be drained, resealed, sanitized.

A day later, the inspector's thin and generic report came through. If I hadn't walked through every room with him, asking questions, learning along the way, the $600 would have been an even greater insult. Although the kitchen was appalling, nothing remediable—appliances were ripped out, the cabinet doors hanging on hinges, mouse and bat feces strewn all over—he graded it "fair" because the completely unusable kitchen sink was still plumbed.

Pete and I discussed 1 Pearl over mushroom pizza on the wharf at the mill, then drove to the east end. We hiked from Point Udall down to Jack and Isaac Reserve, on the rocky trail through the cactus and grasses, and afterwards, swam in a cove on the north coast called Cramer's. Was it then that we fell in love with St. Croix? Might have been.

We drove by a casino that was for sale, and then west, to the other end of island, on the north road, looking for Prosperity—the site of a random piece of land I had put on the 1031 Exchange list. We couldn't get past the locked security gate.

We returned to our favorite cafe every day. We met an elegant, elderly couple, Osborne Fleming and his wife. They owned a transportation company which would come in handy if we wanted to ship down a container of household items and Pete's truck. They told us that a week or two earlier, it had been announced that the refinery was under new ownership and would reopen. We had dodged a bullet. Funny Alice hadn't mentioned it.

A well-groomed young woman often sat at the smaller table against the wall. She worked for the government in legislation. (A couple years later, I found out she worked closely with Congresswoman Stacey Plaskett.) I asked her about the refinery.

"It's not a done deal, but everyone wants it to happen," she said.

"In the paper it says it's moving forward."

"It has one more step before it is finalized, but some are already celebrating. It'll create 700 jobs."

"Local?"

"Most will come in from off-island. And St. Croix shouldn't rely on a single source of employment. We all saw what happened when the refinery closed down in 2012. My father lost his job."

"Will he work there again?"

She looked down at her breakfast. "He passed."

"I'm sorry." I wondered whether if it was refinery-related passing, environmental impacts, but this stoic woman was focused on the health of the economy.

She shook her head.

I was still curious, and trying to understand who was selling 1 Pearl, why this "grand house" was abandoned and by whom. Why had the "seller" line been occupied by three different names over the course of three weeks and was now shared by a couple of litigation lawyers? Who was the artist and where was she painting now? The unsettling feeling of odd legal arrangements and the shared boundary with the refinery and its heavy presence in the western view, and now its imminent reopening, ate away at any vestige of interest and enthusiasm for the property. As much as I loved the physical structure, its mysteries and all that it entailed, I knew I had to walk away.

But it would forever haunt me.

FLAMBOYANT HILL

It was our final day on St. Croix. Still on Zillow's email tickle file, I received notification of every new listing and price adjustment. There seemed to be five a day. I clicked through on many, addict that I am. An unusual stone façade landed in my inbox with this description:

> Originally built by internationally acclaimed photographer, Fritz Henle, this 1+ acre property is now a builder's dream. Set atop a lush, forested crest, this jewel feels like a retreat far from your busy life. Its private, hilltop location is 5 minutes from Sunny Isle, Christiansted & easily accessible to all of St Croix's major roads. Exceptional stone walls flank the sweeping tree-lined driveway, grace the main structure & provide beautiful garden terraces. A gorgeous deep pool, so rare these days, sits astride the master suite & overlooks verdant valleys out to the sea. The unique floor plan is a harmonious blend of indoor/outdoor Caribbean-styled living. This beautiful gem only needs the discerning buyer to bring back its iconic glory. Asking $175,000.

It sounded and looked interesting, and the price was . . . perfect, even though I couldn't do a 1031 Exchange since I'd missed the deadline to declare it. It was so inexpensive it didn't really matter.

We tried to find the property on our way to town. Plugging the address into GPS didn't get us there, although I was pretty sure we were in the right neighborhood, La Grande Princesse. We drove up every private and public "road" that seemed somewhat legit. We made our way up one bumpy dirt lane. At the top, a chain drooped across a driveway that looked uninhabited. A sign said, PRIVATE. This must be it. We got out, locked the car. Barking dogs came racing over, thankfully with wagging tails.

A young woman approached right behind them. "Hello?"

"Hi, we were —" I smiled. I recognized the woman as our waitress from Toast Diner, where we'd eaten brunch the day before. "Hey! We know you!" We told her that we were looking for a house with a pool and stone walls on a hill. We gave her the address and showed her the photos.

She'd grown up on St. Croix, and lived in her grandmother's house behind her. She did not recognize the house in question. We gave up and headed into town for coffee.

We texted Alice about the house. Alice knew the property and said she tried to show it the day before to someone else, but the representing broker had left town and didn't provide a combination for the lockbox. She said there was lots of activity on it. Alice said she used to live there as a young adult, but had no recollection of what it had been like.

 Alice was able to get the lockbox combination and drove us to the same area we had been earlier in the day, and turned into a rutted road cum driveway, over a large flamboyant's roots, and drove a little further and around a bend to where a PVC pipe blocked the driveway. The property was literally across the street from our Toast waitress, but because of its secret entrance and perch, was not visible and unknown.

 Alice jiggled with a lock and chain, and moved the PVC aside. We followed her up a canopied driveway with low stone walls, lined by papaya, mahogany, yucca, turpentine and flamboyant. Around the bend, a couple balled columns welcomed us into a driveway turnaround revealing the skeleton of a house. Through three arches I could see those glazed white tiles in the courtyard I'd seen in every St. Croix listing. Without many walls, half a roof, no windows or doors, the place needed to be reassembled. Layers and layers of tile were excavated and piled, hurled over the stone wall, down the hill, everywhere we looked, evidence of previous lives, inhabitants claiming, re-skinning, making this place theirs.

    We walked through the back "entrance" which led us to the *pièce de résistance*: the cream-colored stone walls near the pool with two enormous window openings framing a small, lush rainforest beyond. And there was a welcome surprise: The other walls were concrete, stripped, scratched, pocked, blotched in shades of gray, "sponged" in chartreuse, dripping with sea-foam green or the splotches of tile glue— and gorgeous. They were works of art, abstract expressionist, each wall unique. Those walls in the front half of the house would remain as they were, untouched, unpainted, raw, "natural" as the locals said. And it was my job to save them from someone who would paint over them. The main house also had terrazzo floors and the remaining roof was concrete, squared and flat-ish, with large overhangs and mid-century lines. A courtyard between the two structures created a Mediterranean feel.

    The second, back part of the house was a puzzling array of walls, many dismantled, all connected to a single, long, tall wall. Beyond that wall was a neighbor's lawn, and house. (When I peered around the corner a couple months later, I saw a man by the front door cradling a large gun on his lap. It turned out to be Governor Bryan's personal home; he had just been elected. Henceforth, we called that side of the house the Governor's Side.)

    We fell in love with this project—1031 be damned. Not only had the house been Henle's, it had magic all its own. There was something about it, perched on a hill with long views, a big sky, a western vista. The interior courtyard was intimate and personal. An enormous, sculptural flamboyant tree with orange blossoms in full bloom shaded an adjacent brick patio a few steps down. Another half dozen flamboyants lined the driveway. The sun was going down as we paced through and around this fabulous ruin.

    It was a steal for an entire acre on a forested hillside. It was not in the tony east end, where most of the (white) retirees tuck away in condos or in private coves and vista-ed hills, but it also didn't have the refinery in its sunset like 1 Pearl. I don't want to believe we loved it more because of the association with Henle, the celebrity connection. But because of Henle, I projected a thoughtful aesthetic, logical choices and I trusted the bones.

    We decided we didn't need an inspector to tell us that everything would need to be redone. Would he assure us that the house wouldn't tumble down the hill? Or, once filled, the pool would?

    When we got back to the States, distance tempered my enthusiasm. Here I was, with the proceeds from a house I'd renovated and sold in the Hudson Valley to simplify my life, ready to throw in a bid on a challenging project I'd seen for half an hour, one I would never be undertaking on my own, as a single woman on an island where I knew no one. There was no way I would have arrived there without Pete.

So, before I lobbed in a bid, I asked Pete to commit to buying the property from me if our relationship ended. Pete was, after all, the one who wanted a house in the sun, but couldn't yet free up the cash from his marriage. He agreed, and wrote me an email stating that he would purchase the house for the sales price plus any subsequent investment. He also agreed to go down and start pulling things together in November, so we could spend Christmas there with family. (Ha! What were we thinking? It ended up taking a year—not a month—for the house to be partially livable, and an additional year to get the pool in working order.)

The sellers were breaking up and selling the property —which they'd owned for a year. Alice wrote, "Listing is being shown about 5 times a day for the last 3 days. I have shown it 4 times already!" Next I knew, they had an accepted offer; mine became backup. Alice started to push 1 Pearl again.

The first buyer backed out, so my offer was next in line. We went back and forth a couple times and landed on $164,500. I printed, signed, scanned and re-sent the paperwork.

A couple days went by while we waited for the sellers to sign.

"He's a real ass," wrote Alice when the Offer to Purchase was delayed unexpectedly. "Jill's sweet. I know her from high school." I asked Alice if there were any plans or photos of the house before they took it apart, maybe even the way Henle had originally conceived of the house. Alice sent me some old listings; two were informative.

In 2004, it was on the market for $405,000. The older pictures showed a dowdy, closed-in house, cobbled together, with loads of breeze block in what were now the dramatic, large openings. I never would have been interested in it had I seen the earlier photos. In 2017, it was on the market for $109,000 (Alice: *bank sale!*). The sellers made a tidy little profit on me, although the demolition likely cost them a penny and time. At a minimum, it cost them their relationship.

I asked Alice to find out where the cisterns and septic were.

Both brokers invoked that I could have had a contingency, an inspection. This wasn't a legal matter and I wasn't backing out. I just sought basic information as the almost new owner. If I were the seller, I would be happy to provide it to a buyer. Eventually, the seller's broker wrote that there were three cisterns, and the septic was under the driveway, which was later confirmed by a plumber, who recognized the place from years ago. In fact, over the years, it seems that many people knew the house in all its iterations—unlike with 1 Pearl.

Six weeks after stepping on St. Croix, after seeing the property for thirty minutes at sunset, I owned Henle's home on the hill.

A week after closing, Pete and I were back on the island pacing, planning, assessing, lining up contractors, deciding what was going to be a bedroom and which was the living room, whether we needed two bathrooms or the three that sort-of existed (I assumed I

should stick with the current drains), where walls would be rebuilt, where doors and windows would fill openings, whether the hall was too narrow and needed to be widened by taking down a closet wall, and would it matter that it no longer lined up with the door opposite. (Yes, but what to do?) I tried to discern and incorporate the previous owners' intentions from drawings scrawled on the walls. Sometimes I did something else, but left the drawing, such as *TOILET HERE?* Would the kitchen go where we thought it had been in the 1970s, on the Governor's Side in a bizarre location with extremely low ceilings, or where SINK was chalked near the pool? Decisions were domino, and not easy. There was no discernible logic to the layout, and some serious challenges. Every room had two to three doorways, which made bed placement a challenge. What had this place looked like when it was originally conceived? How much was the result of years of additions and muddled thinking? It was all such a jumble.

*   *   *

Across from Twin Cities Coffee, where we'd been many times, we saw a sign: HENLE Photography. How had we not seen it before?

We approached and pulled out a brochure from a plastic holder. Tina Henle, daughter of Fritz, was an event photographer and had a gallery up the stairs, open by appointment. Within minutes, I emailed Tina. I explained we had just bought her father's home and we'd love to meet her. She wrote back saying she wasn't on island, but to call her brother Martin.

Martin answered. "Yea. I saw that. I don't know how they claimed that was my dad's house. I live in my dad's house. I had meant to contact the realtor." Fritz Henle had a compound in neighboring Little Princess. "Maybe they claimed it was his because his first wife owned it," he posited. There didn't seem room in the conversation to gain greater clarity on whether she owned it before or after they were married, but it was clear that the house was not Fritz's. He had little to nothing to do with it. We agreed to meet another time, but never did. I found out what I was—and was not—looking for.

The following day, we circled back to 1 Pearl to see how it looked with an infusion of rain and a little distance. It had been six weeks. We tried the lock at the gate; Alice had said the combination was her birth year. I guessed her age and it popped. When we walked through the house, we noticed the mouse and bat-infested kitchen had been cleaned up, and the debris in the garage had been removed.

When I mentioned my findings regarding the provenance of the house to Alice, she was outraged. "I would never list something until I did my research! You should go look for the property's history at the Recorder of Deeds, City Hall, in Christiansted." The onus was on me.

Pete dropped me off at City Hall en route to the Gallow's Bay hardware store. I had to leave my phone at the front desk, so I wouldn't be able to reach Pete, or our plumber, who was supposed to come by that afternoon. I also wouldn't be able to photograph the records but would have to copy everything by hand.

I entered through an elegant, manicured courtyard and headed right into an air-conditioned, low-ceilinged office with a grumpy door. The helpful folks behind the desk showed me how things worked: You start with the most recent volume for a specific neighborhood, and within that book look for the address, and most recent transaction, then step back in time, as the deed transfered from one owner to another. They showed me where to find the previous books, until the beginning of time. I consulted several until the trail led me to the earliest records I could find. For my property, it stopped—or began—with Jose Bermudez Heyliger and Anne Bermudez purchasing the property by Warranty Deed in July 1964 from Manuel Viera. They resold it in May 1965 to another party—that is, a year later. Something didn't make sense. I vowed to return to see if I missed something. There was no mention of Henle, or Atti, for that matter.

While I was there, I looked up the abandoned, buried-in-the-bush house below mine which I thought I should try to purchase, since it was so close. With his name in hand, I found the last owner's obituary in the local paper online. I reached out to one or two of the relatives and friends mentioned in the obituary but never heard back. It was likely stuck in probate, like many abandoned island properties.

I also looked up 1 Pearl, to see if it in fact went back to the Knights of Malta, as Alice claimed. I was sent from one old leather-bound book to another, unwinding time, each more frayed than the previous, with entries written in blue fountain pen in the script of yesteryear, but never got to 1 Pearl's origins. I got close but ran out of time.

I decided to write the seller's broker, and copy Alice, inquiring about my property's provenance, which didn't square with the listing's description. She wrote back that one of the sellers was a personal friend of the Henle family and it was confirmed information, that I should have done my due diligence before I purchased the property. I privately debated how much Henle's association had swayed me in the purchase. Mostly I wondered about the ethics of misrepresentation.

When I asked whether the family friend was Martin, she wrote, *no, Jahn*. I found mention of a *Jan* in Fritz's obituary, February 5, 1993, in *The New York Times*.

> Fritz Henle, a prolific freelance photographer renowned for his stylish travel pictures, died on Sunday at Teachers Hospital in San Juan, P.R. He was 83 and lived in St. Croix, V.I. His son, Martin, said the cause of death was heart failure.
>
> Mr. Henle was born in Dortmund, Germany, and studied photography in Munich before coming to the United States in 1936. He soon began to do freelance assignments for magazines including Life, Mademoiselle, Holiday and Harper's Bazaar. He became widely known for his classically composed black-and-white images. . . . Mr. Henle moved to the Virgin Islands from New York in 1948. He photographed throughout the Caribbean, and in 1972 he published a portfolio of pictures taken in the Virgin Islands. . . . In addition to his son Martin, of St. Croix, he is survived by his wife, Marguerite; two daughters, Tina and Maria, of St. Croix; another son, Jan, of New York City and Puerto Rico, and a sister, Anne Marie Pope of Washington.

I found Jan Henle's artist website. It showed a longstanding art project underway in Puerto Rico, a living sculpture, *Con el Mismo Amor,* in the mountains of southwestern Puerto Rico near the town of Maricao, three hours from San Juan. Although also connected to photography, and photographing women earlier in his career, Jan's work broke from his father's in that his photos were sensual depictions of earth and landscape. They are in collections all over the world, including the Metropolitan Museum of Art, Colby College (I remember seeing a triptych when I was there for my nephew's graduation before I ever set foot on St. Croix) and many others. I contacted him.

Jan's wife Dee wrote back from New York, saying that Jan was in Puerto Rico without WIFI or a computer, but he did have a cell phone. He weathered Hurricanes Irma and Maria and was rebuilding.

She mentioned that the house I purchased was "actually Jan's mother Atti's house."

I called Jan the next day. "Hello, Jan?" I pronounced *J* as a *Y*. "Am I saying your name correctly, like in German? Or is it *Jan*?" with a hard J.

"Yes, *Yan*. It's Dutch." Henle was German; his mother Atti van den Berg was Dutch. After I reintroduced myself, and my reason for calling, he explained, "My mother built that house herself. She moved to Saint Croix in 1952 when I was four years old, after divorcing Fritz."

"So, Fritz, your father, never lived there? He didn't build it?"

"They may have owned the property — the land — together, but he never lived there and had nothing to do with the house. You are lucky it was Atti's house and not Fritz's. She's much more interesting." He went on to describe Atti, a dancer from Holland, who founded a welcoming dance studio drawing from many ethnicities and dance forms. Jan, too, danced in his youth.

"Fritz followed her to Saint Croix?"

"He came later. He said he wanted to see more of me." I sensed doubt in his voice.

According to Jan, Atti contracted a (possibly) Argentinian architect to build the original core dwelling, a concrete "cottage." While the house I purchased was not large, it didn't feel like a cottage, rather a sprawling Mediterranean retreat. But one of the things I adored was the rough roof line of a house—likely the original cottage— within the house. I later called the Department of Planning & Natural Resources (DPNR), where building plans are submitted and permits issued, to see if they had any architectural renderings, but was told they throw away everything after three years.

"If you're standing west and looking into the hill, in the patio door, the kitchen is to the left." Yes! Where SINK was scrawled under the window, where I intended to put the sink. "There's a small bathroom." Check! I would keep the many layers of tile glue in that bathroom as they were.

"Later, two small bedrooms were built in the car port for me and my brother." Were these the two small rooms near the retaining wall on the Governor's Side? Or the single room with a low ceiling which became my bedroom, which had, admittedly, a garage-like feel? From his description, I couldn't figure out where the main bedroom had been. The stone walls, and huge windows, the principle architectural feature of the house, did not exist, nor did the Governor's Side, at Atti's time. The core structure near the pool had architectural integrity and was solid concrete, including the roof, and had the terrazzo tile floors of that era, but because they extended into the living room, beyond the cottage, I inferred, may have come later.

"Was the terrazzo there?" I asked.

"As a fourteen year old, I'm not sure I knew or cared much about the floors. . . . My grandmother lived in another cottage down the hill, built by the same architect." That could be the abandoned house in the brush directly below. "I built myself a house on another plot, also a little cottage. I'm sure that's been all built up and looks nothing like it did. Originally, we had five acres. . . . Jill— is it? —Wilson called me about a year ago to ask about the house. I think she was one of my mother's students."

When I spoke to Jan, there was no ambiguity in his answer or memory. In fact, while the dates differed, I was amazed throughout our conversation of his recollection of events. How had Jan's conversation with Jill led to a claim that Fritz Henle built the home?

I am not an archaeologist or a vole, but I dig. Why did I need to know about the Henles and Atti? I was no longer looking for house plans or verification of who built the house but piecing together the story of a remarkable woman and her progeny, connected to a well-known man. The search began innocently enough, assuming a "prolific photographer" might have left pictures of the home he'd built, a possible blueprint for its reconstruction.

"I had a difficult childhood. I didn't get along with my stepfather, or my stepmother. She was jealous of me, I think, the attention my father gave me." According to an article in *The St Thomas Source,* August 20, 2020, about the closing of the Henle gallery in Christiansted, two years after I arrived on St. Croix:

> It was in 1947 when [Fritz's} flight to Venezuela for an outdoor fashion shoot was curtailed, he ventured to St. Croix instead. At Sprat Hall, he met Marguerite, who became his model for his exquisite fashion work, and later his wife and the mother of their three children.

Martin, Tina and Marie Henle came from Fritz's second marriage to Marguerite. Fritz's meeting of Marguerite in St. Croix would have been just before Jan was born in New York City to Atti, in 1948. Yet, in Marguerite's obituary, it states that she arrived on St. Croix in 1952. Perhaps they were both just visiting when they met; otherwise, the critical dates that would elucidate the tangled romances did not align. I found multiple photographs by Fritz of Marguerite posing nude in 1953. According to the *The St. Thomas Source,* Feb. 13, 2007, Fritz and Marguerite's first child Maria was born September 22, 1955.

When I returned to the Recorder of Deeds Office, and the Cadastral Office, for a second and third time in February 2025, I did a broader search. The records show that Fritz and Atti bought 5.3 acres of 89 La Grande Princesse in July 1951. Anne Henle (Atti) received it by Quitclaim Deed from Fritz in March/April 1955 "conveying all his right title and interest in this plot for $1.00 and other good and valuable considerations," likely as part of their 1954 divorce. In March 1958, Pepe and Atti got a mortgage for the acreage, possibly to build the house. Rancher Hans Lawaetz remembers Atti and Pepe living at Annaly Farms at some point, maybe in the 1955-58 period, before the house was built, while Pepe worked on the ranch. Part of the initial confusion was that Atti van den Berg went by Anne Bermudez, Anne Bermudez Heyliger and Anne Henle, but everyone I met referred to her as *Atti*.

A couple advertisements in *The Saint Croix Avis* from the mid-sixties appeared in an online search in which Bermudez-Heyliger is selling houses, likely the five acres in pieces. The ad shown here is from October 2, 1965, but I found several, with different plot sizes. None matched the acreage of the place I'd purchased. But the second one in this ad describes 1.34 acres "bearing grafted grapefruit, orange, persian limes, tangerines and avocadoes," which may have included my plot and the property below. I like to believe that Pepe's landscaping touch is evident in the loosely curated, terraced, mini tropical forest sloping away from my home, although from a sustenance point of view, I had only a single banana tree which died in 2022.

"Is there a lot of violence on the island?" I asked Jan.

"St. Croix, when I was growing up, had no violence. I didn't know what race was. My friends were Black. It was the war that changed things." Although USVI citizens couldn't vote, they were drafted. "Blacks came back angry," Jan said. This led to racial unrest and violent activism. And in the sixties and seventies there were lots of homicides, and, unlike today, many were across racial lines.

I first learned about the Fountain Valley Massacre from Jan. Annaly Farms, where Pepe worked, became part of Rockefeller's Fountain Valley Golf Course, now Carambola. In 1972, five armed men killed eight employees and golfers in an execution-style shooting. All but one of the victims was white. Much has been written about the brutal massacre; a documentary was made. The shooters were war veterans and likely suffered from PTSD, not yet a named affliction. Nixon and Agnew, who both had homes on the golf course, along with many others, fled the island; tourism plummeted.

A few months later, when I went out for a bite, bringing a book to read on the Fountain Valley Massacre, I bumped into a couple at the bar who were visiting from Boston. We chatted for a bit. He had grown up on St. Croix. He looked over at my book, and said that his father, Warren Young, had presided over the 1973 Fountain Valley trial.

I looked up from my bowl of pasta at the man more closely. "Did you happen to go to school in Boston?"

"Yes."

"Class of 83?"

"Yes." He smiled. "Cindy?"

"Tim?" We were college classmates. Since our meeting, we get together every year when he and his family come down for a break from the Boston winters. Tim is a font of information on the island's history and people and wildly entertaining. Tim grew up in the neighborhood and knew the house I had purchased as a youngster, but doesn't remember much by way of detail.

After my conversation with Jan, Jan's wife Dee sent me Atti's biography including her many contributions to the dance world, from touring as a solo dancer, performing on Broadway, to founding Theater Dance, both in New York and later in St. Croix, among the first racially-mixed dance companies, integrating workshops by internationally-acclaimed dancers. "She was an early practitioner of labanotation, a system of recording movement on paper."

Atti and Pepe moved to Puerto Rico in 1986. Along with dance, Atti pursued painting. Jan and Dee sent me her art portfolio. I was blown away by the paintings' sophistication and originality, which had a dose of surrealism, at once dark and whimsical. Beloved Atti died in 2003, but she is remembered fondly by her students, some of whom I have come across on St. Croix's dance floors.

I noted, "You moved to Puerto Rico, like your stepfather."

Jan explained, "The Caribbean is a part of you. . . I haven't been back to St. Croix in 18 years but when people ask me where I'm from, I say St. Croix. It's where I grew up."

Jan's childhood seemed painful. While he clearly adored his mother, he had little to say about Fritz, other than *he was very focused on his photography*. He hadn't spoken to his step siblings in decades.

"My mother and father always had a good relationship," he reiterated, but it seemed the other permutations didn't work, perhaps because theirs did.

Jan thought he recognized my name, that I was a dancer, maybe a student of his mother's, like Jill. I spelled out my last name. Although I love to dance, and loved the idea that I now owned the house of this tremendous dancer, I couldn't imagine someone with my name was a professional dancer in New York. I later learned of a renowned choreographer, Cynthia Oliver, who fit the description.

I thanked Jan and Dee for sharing so much of themselves and rich history with me. I returned with renewed excitement to my challenging project on a bluff in St. Croix, honored to be the custodian of Atti's home.

A couple years later, I met Jill Wilson, one of the previous owners, at a fundraiser. As Jan mentioned, Jill had been a student of Atti's and had run a dance studio herself with her then-husband. In fact, one of the reasons she bought the house is because it belonged to her beloved mentor.

When Jill visited after I had made the house inhabitable, she brought with her and gifted me a small watercolor by Atti. I hung it in a protected but visible spot in the house. I wished I'd met Jill earlier, before I'd had to puzzle through things on my own, to ask what their plans had been, and how the house was before they'd dismantled it, or when Atti inhabited it. Jill seemed to love what I had done, although her vision had been very different from my own. I hosted a half dozen gatherings at my house for Jill and her friends, I think to show them that she hadn't been crazy. When I saw the real estate listing of the house she had purchased, I realized I never would have purchased it, even in foreclosure. It was a clogged, dark mess. It was their stripping it down that revealed its potential.

THE RESURRECTION

I broke up with Pete. A jealous sort, he had become more and more paranoid, depressed and belligerent as he reduced his anti-depressants without doctor supervision. He rarely let me out of his sight, even to go to the bathroom, although I begged him for privacy. He was with me 24/7 with nothing to do. I asked him to bring an art project to work on, or leave for a bit, and come back. He would text me that he was depressed within minutes. He threw tantrums in public places, and at Thanksgiving, multiple times, in front of my family, in his pajamas, like a three-year-old. I decided I'd had enough of his erratic behavior.

He handled the break up with his usual grace, flooding my phone with provocative threats and insults and then asked if I still wanted to go to Asia with him, for example. He threatened to visit St. Croix over Christmas with his son, when he knew I would be there, even though he had no reason to be there but to intimidate me. It was confusing and scary and convinced me that I had made the right decision. When I showed my phone to a woman who runs a domestic violence center, who I happened to sit next to at a dinner, she took one glance, declared him abusive, and advised me to not respond.

But before I blocked him, I half-heartedly asked Pete to buy the house in St. Croix from me as he had promised he would. I was intrigued yet overwhelmed by the prospect of going through the enormous renovation on my own. At first he ignored the request, and then reneged, saying that he'd meant he would buy it only if he broke up with me, not if I broke up with him. So I was stuck with a ruin on St. Croix, on an island where I knew no one, as a single woman. I hadn't even heard yet how dangerous it can be. Friends flippantly told me to turn around and resell it. But I didn't want to take a loss of tens of thousands of dollars. And I was already emotionally invested in the project. There was no going back.

*   *   *

I have renovated a half dozen homes over the years, but not one like this. This ramshackle skeleton required everything— roof, windows, doors, walls, plumbing, electrical—and immediately, if I wanted to get out ahead of hurricane season. The first order of business was to close the roof and to simultaneously repair, clean and seal the cisterns. Electrical couldn't go in until there was a roof. Windows and doors needed to be in before June so a hurricane wouldn't blow off the new roof. I needed architectural drawings and building permits and approvals.

Pete had sent an old, arthritic long-bed truck to the island —spending more on the transport than the truck was worth—and it was still on route. I ended up buying it from

him and using it that first year. It was useful, and, I have to admit, I enjoyed riding around in my Island Truck as if I were an Island Girl. But it reminded me of him. I cursed him every time I struggled to shift the gears and pumped more air into the tires. I unloaded it as soon as the bulk of the work was done. I didn't want Pete parked in the driveway.

Arriving a year after Hurricanes Maria and Irma, I competed for scarce and expensive tradesmen and materials, as FEMA pumped millions into the island's repair. Lots of people needed new roofs, not just me, and arguably with greater urgency. I met with dozens of plumbers, electricians, masons, painters, gardeners, landscapers, pest and pool guys. We agreed on prices and scope of work and then they didn't show. But I learned from every conversation, asking lots of questions. To get a jump-start, I brought two carpenters from the Hudson Valley for the month of January. One had never been on a plane before; the other had never been out of the country. I shepherded them through the airport in their wife-beaters and steel-toed boots just after the New Year. Because there was no electricity, we got by with loud, annoying, gas-fueled, anti-environmental generators to operate the tools. One broke down. Then another. I borrowed my neighbor's generator, and it croaked too; I paid them $400 to replace it. Nonetheless, we banged out the roof, and covered critical openings in short order. We had our laughs and our challenges, with me acting as their chauffeur and Home Depot runner. I must have loaded 500 bags of concrete into the back of that old pickup. It was a memorable, productive month.

Operating as general contractor and architect, I quickly boned up on what it means to build a hurricane-proof, water-catching roof. Ducts and conduits transport the precious water which arrives during the rainy season into a couple of cisterns below the house. We created an aqueduct that brought the water from the Governor's Side to the two larger cisterns below the main house.

The plentiful and enormous openings which drew me to the home were so large and numerous that there was not enough wall to accommodate hurricane shutters. The Dade-County hurricane-approved louvre windows I eventually went with would double as security. I had assumed that the hurricanes were responsible for the house's condition but later learned that the sellers had deliberately stripped the house of years and layers of tile and "bandages," including the roof. I hauled all the broken mosaic and concrete block in five-gallon plastic buckets, up a set of stairs and out to the truck. Carrying roughly fifty pounds, I clocked six miles that day. I sorted and used nail-less, non-sharp concrete rubble to fill potholes in the driveway, and drove the rest to the dump.

Over time, I assembled a team of mostly locals—local to the Caribbean, that is. They came from Antigua, Dominica, Trinidad, Jamaica, Puerto Rico, Dominican Republic, Nevis and St. Croix. I valued them highly and they became dear to me as I ferried them back and forth in the pickup to Jiffy Mart in Christiansted. They competed to ride in the front seat since the backseat had little leg room. They had sick or disabled spouses or lived alone as migrant day laborers. A couple had stands at the local farmer's market. One took a half day on Friday to collect fruit and vegetables from "the bush." They shared local foods and plant knowledge with me, along with trade expertise. I often worked alongside them.

We squared and fenced the three round arches in the driveway. This wall became the main entry, separating the turnaround from the inner courtyard physically and visually. I jackhammered five inches of concrete and standard issue glazed white tile out of that patio—which oddly had at one time been enclosed—to reveal additional terrazzo. The main house and the guest wing are now joined by this terrazzo patio, possibly the original design, where there is an outdoor bar and multiple entertaining and living spaces. A large, sculptural flamboyant tree shades a brick patio a few steps below. The deep pool on the west side of the house, a breeding ground for mosquitoes and tadpoles when I arrived, required significant investment to bring up to code, worth every penny. With a big sky, it offers another outdoor "room" to sip morning coffee (which I eventually brewed at home), catch sunsets, and view the hemisphere of a rainbow after a shower. A fence, thoughtfully scaled and joining the existing walls, steps around the entire house, giving the property dimension and security, and keeps my dog Dexter nearby.

After the roof to the carport was reconstructed, we installed an above ground cistern, or "buffalo," to catch that roof's water, to top off the pool or water plants.

In the reconstruction, I employed my usual tenets of minimalism and sustainability not just in the result but in the journey. I reuse and re-purpose. I see how the sun works its way around the house, and in this case, how to harness the hilltop breeze to minimize Caribbean heat and spring mold. We plastered and painted the exterior of the house in inviting tropical colors—salmon and turmeric with a neutral khaki trim, like the fence. In contrast, the inside of the main house was left "natural" and raw. We did what was necessary for structural integrity—such as chipping out and sealing rusted rebar—but left rough, unfinished edges and graffiti, imprints of old bathroom tile, some tinted mustard, or green, or gray with squiggles. Each wall has its own palette and is—in my estimation— a work of art. Some internal walls don't reach the ceiling, a feature I saw designed into old plantation houses to allow circulation among rooms.

I located elusive but island-lexicon glass block and used it to create a tub and a shower stall and to fill several superfluous openings, thus allowing natural light to reach interior rooms, maintaining the open feel as when I first saw the structure. Years later, I found two hand-blown glass sinks on Facebook marketplace. One was installed in the outdoor bar area, the other in the small bathroom, floating atop glass blocks and plumbed with raw copper plumbing and outdoor spigots.

Another principle I subscribe to is flexibility, rather than, say, dedicated spaces or built-ins. Living spaces are multiple rather than single use. With daybeds throughout, and flexible partitions, there is ample room for guests. A nap on the four-poster palm tree king

bed in the living room is an afternoon treat.

For an island notorious for expensive electricity and frequent outages, my electric bill runs about $100 a month. My appliances are all ENERGY STAR and I dragged down a highly-efficient 90-pound variable pool pump from the States in a suitcase. During the day, I rarely turn on a light. With large, well-placed windows, shade, and a gentle zephyr which wafts through the house, especially at night, there is no need for air conditioning. Ceiling and mobile fans suffice in a pinch. In the end, the two 80" X 120" windows in the main living areas have only a large screen—no glass. I couldn't imagine closing out the natural world, my own tropical rainforest, beyond. We made hurricane doors out of repurposed corrugated metal roofing found on the side of the road, which we install when I leave for the summer. Sixteen mahogany louvre doors, from the back aisle of Home Depot, integrate the spaces visually.

I shipped a container of furniture from New York, including sofa mattresses and daybeds designed by industrial designer Ward Bennett, pulled from my NYC apartment before I sold it; a five-foot square dining room table; ten BBDW Ladder and Square Guest

Chairs left behind, half-finished as seconds in a warehouse, which a friend and I completed using speaker wire, felt, jute webbing, string, plywood—each different; vintage chests stacked as a coffee table; a collection of antique pastel-hued porcelain pitchers; Marimekko butterfly chairs; five lanky St. Claire mid-century wooden and brass table lamps; sleek, inexpensive kitchen IKEA cabinetry; outdoor furniture; and my own art. I supplement from estate sales where Danish mid-century pieces can be found if the sellers have lived on St. Croix for decades: mahogany live-edge side tables, a classic Dansk ice bucket. Blue-green fishing nets and cords collected (to alleviate impact on wildlife) on Ha' Penny beach decorate the living room stone wall. Leftover concrete blocks are reissued as toilet paper holders, in keeping with the vocabulary of the deconstructed home. Concrete cores removed from the walls of the pool when it was plumbed are used as doorstops.

From a roofless, wall-less, windowless, door-less ramshackle ruin perched on a hill, an open, breezy mid-century modern retreat was born. I called it Flamboyant Hill.

* * *

Large hermit crabs lived below the house between the cistern and pool when I first moved in. I found them a tad disconcerting as I explored the nooks and crannies of the underworld. One of the first nights I spent in my home, without electricity or running water, I heard a loud knock at the door. I jumped out of bed petrified, alert, wondering who had found me on the hill, in the dark. I opened the door and peeked out, and then down. An enormous hermit crab outside had been throwing himself against the door.

When I told my mason, Henry, about it in the morning, he said, "Oh, yeah. They like to snuggle at night."

Since I've moved in, they've moved on. I hope they've found somewhere cozy.

THE RUSTY TANK

The driver climbed out of the truck loaded with lumber. "I ask you whether you live near *aslfkjaskld;jsdklfj*. . . ." He was shaking his head. His tone was frustrated but not angry, and he had a significant stutter and a strong Caribbean accent to my new-to-island ears.

"I'm sorry? I'm a little hard of hearing," I said. He repeated himself a couple more times, but I just couldn't make out what he was saying.

"Come," he said, beckoning with his hand. I followed him to the edge of the turn-around. He pointed down the hill.

In the distance below, an oversized blue metal tank sat where the roads came together in a T, not far from the base of the private road the house perched on—if you call the rough and tumble dirt shared driveway a private road.

"It was painted blue, but they still call it de rusty tank."

Oh. "The rusty tank! Next time!" I smiled.

So, I learned to direct future visits and delivery men by starting with, *you know the rusty tank?*

No one knew Rattan Road, and it wasn't part of my plot address. The intersection of route 81 meant nothing either, even though signs indicated 81 was the neck part of the T. Five Corners was the other landmark I knew and referenced. It was all coming together: Coming from Christiansted, take a left at 5 Corners. Glass 2000 on your left. Go about a mile…towards but before you hit the rusty tank.

I drove by the rusty tank many times a day, and it was a comforting if not industrial presence, part of the neighborhood. But I hadn't appreciated its fame.

It was blue, that is, what peeked through the graffiti.

Kim + Stacy.

N. Y.

Hearts.

A few other hard-to-make-out bubble-gum, colorful scrawls. About twelve feet high and ten feet in diameter, it wasn't clear what the tank originally contained. Water? Oil? But now it had a purpose. The rusty tank was my landmark.

St. Croix was one of the leading producers of sugar in the 18th century, with some 186 plantations which became neighborhoods, which translate roughly into physical addresses, and a plot number—not to be confused with a mailing address, which could be a post office box, or an array of boxes down your small roadway in the closest neighborhood. The old stone structures—sugar mills and plantation Great Houses—that still exist are a constant reminder of the plantation history. Neighborhood names include estates such as Prosperity, Judith's Fancy, Serendipity, Catherine's Hope, Welcome, Grapetree Eb, Pearl, Whim and La Grande Princesse, where my house is. Many are known, and descriptive, have connotations of one sort or another, which will take me years to decipher. Some are now gated communities. Your neighborhood may tell people a little bit about you, the way Upper East Side or Williamsburg might if you lived in New York City. Landmarks tell people how to find you.

When I first came down to St. Croix to work on my ruin, I stayed at an Airbnb. After three weeks, there was a roof, some doors and windows, but no electricity or proper plumbing. My furniture had arrived via container (early! too early!) and was piled high under dusty tarps. I decided to save some money by camping in the living room, while the carpenters still slept at another Airbnb. We had stacked all the mattresses on top of one another, so I decided to play Princess and the Pea, sleeping atop all four of them. I set up everything before I left for the evening, so I wouldn't have to find things later in the dark without lights. I dug out some sheets and pillows and made my bed. I lay out my toothbrush and water, a flashlight, nightwear.

I had water in the cistern, just no plumbing. One of my workers had hooked up a water pump in the cistern, so all I had to do was turn on the generator to take a hose shower. I got the soap and towel ready to take a cold shower in broad daylight on the hill, in view of a distant neighbor no doubt. It turned out the cistern guys had drained the water earlier in the day and disconnected the downspout. The "shower" I had been counting on was not in the offing.

I was filthy and didn't have time to go to the beach for a saltwater "bath" which is what I often did other evenings. I would use the water captured off the roof the day before. I had propped a (new) trashcan under a downspout that used to be connected to a small cistern I had recently discovered. The guys had been using the water to mix cement and rinse their hands, but I had no option. Most of the silt had settled. I jumped into the trashcan and took a sponge bath, supplemented by disposable wipes. I put on mascara and lipstick using the rusty mirror in the small bathroom on the Governor Side, and changed into a blue jean skirt and fresh top. I was ready to go to Jump Up, a kind of block party in town.

That night, the carpenters had rented their own Jeep and went off on their own, although I found out later, they'd done exactly what we'd done together before. I guess they needed to do it by themselves, without me, regardless of how fun I thought I was. I had told them about Jump Up, which I thought they would have enjoyed, with live music and food trucks, and everyone milling about, but they ignored me and headed out west to Rainbow in Frederiksted. My own body was fatigued from jackhammering much of the day, much of the month, so I went to Jump Up on the early side. And without electricity, there wasn't much to do in the dark at the construction site.

I walked around the stalls, ducking into stores and sampling some Louisiana-style gumbo and a scoop each of tamarind and ginger ice cream. Bands were set up on every street corner and in between. Smoke from grills and spotlights punctuated the meanderings. I bumped into a few people I knew among the throngs of roaming tourists and locals. After

the Moko Jumbies filled the streets and me with awe, I headed home.

This would be my first night sleeping at the house. I used my phone to find the key to open the front door, to illuminate my passage. I brushed my teeth with bottled water and spit into the driveway. I used a face wipe on my face and hands. I changed. I slipped into the clean sheets. Mmm. It felt nice. I felt the breeze and heard the night sounds I knew would be there, that hadn't been at the Airbnb I'd been staying for the past three weeks.

I was happy to be surrounded by this nocturnal concert, and, at first, it seemed, as I'd hoped, mosquitoes were not an issue, even with no screens in the gaping openings. I certainly wasn't thinking about rats and snakes or Cuban white frogs or centipedes yet.

I was exhausted, but I couldn't sleep.

I lay awake following individual croaks and bellows, trying to ascertain whether they were frogs or birds. One *had* to be a frog at the bottom of my almost-empty green pool water.

The first hour was just about excitement.

The second hour was about pain and exhaustion. I used to miss the feeling of muscle fatigue I remembered from my childhood. Sore muscles were reminders of hours playing kick-the-can and tag. But tonight, my whole body screamed from the jackhammering I'd been doing with such determination the entire month, trying to get the most out of my $22/day tool rental. I wondered whether I was doing permanent damage to my nerves, whether my hands were just a bundle of fractures. My legs, too, were heavy and pulsing. I couldn't sleep because I was in so much pain, throbbing. I had no idea where my Advil was, and I wouldn't rummage in the dust and dark to find it.

I tried counting to six, three long counts in, three long counts out, meditation-like breathing. I put a pillow beneath my knees when I lay on my back to ease lower back pain, and between my knees when I lay on my side to pad the knocking bones.

That third hour, with few screens, the mosquitoes finally discovered me, just as I discovered sleep. I waited until one was right near my ear and then smacked it. I listened. The whine was gone, replaced by ringing. I sprayed myself with poison and hoped for the best. I pulled the sheet over my face and head until it got so hot, I kicked it all off and lay one leg in the open. I was hot then cold, then I just wanted the weight of the covers on my body again. This cycle repeated dozens of times.

My friend Mary Beth texted. "Where are you?" They were still at the Jump Up dancing to Schindler, an amazing one-man band musical act. She wanted me to come back and dance with her. I texted her that I'd gone to bed early. I tried to resist checking my phone but did for the next half hour.

Just as I was drifting into sleep close to midnight, I heard, vaguely, a hollow, loud BANG! like large metal impact. I had only heard that sound a few times before in my life. I was a little too groggy to speculate, but then awoke to sirens. I got up and walked out to the edge of the pool. From there, I could see down to the T, to the rusty tank. The whole

area was ablaze in circulating, pulsing emergency lights. The blue and red and white lights turned to blue an hour later, after the ambulances left. The police cars remained for hours.

At Twin Cities Coffee House the next morning a man was talking about the accident. Two cars crashed into one another. Two people died.

"Young people! They drive so fast and reckless!"

I found out weeks later that they were new employees of the re-opened refinery, that they'd rented the jeep from a friend of my neighbors, not an official rental office. And now the jeep owners were being sued by the parents of the dead drivers.

On the way back from my latte, I drove to the intersection. The rusty tank was on its side. A huge gash revealed rusty bars, like ribs, inside. The impact had torn the tank from the ground to reveal a concrete underbelly. That must have been some impact. I wanted to take a picture but didn't want to cause another accident. There seemed to be more traffic than usual. Then I realized, they too had come to take pictures of the beloved rusty tank.

That was the first night I spent in my new home.

BEES AND BATTERIES

On a late afternoon August day, I was dropped off by a group taxi at my "house"— really still a construction site—after being away since April. The house was partially enclosed, with a temporary electric meter and no running water. At first glance, it all seemed to be the way I left it. But as I looked around, in between the two buildings, I heard a loud hum. On closer — but not too close — inspection, I spotted a large, dark, active mass: a swarm of bees in an opening between two stones in the foundation. I couldn't tell how deep they went and how many there were. Although contained, the swarm was a living organism, and very present. Portentous.

I located the list of contractors the realtor had given me when I bought the house and scrolled to Pest Control.

I called Bee Man.

I called Oliver Exterminators.

I called Honey Man.

Honey Man called back and said he could come by the following morning. "It'll cost $250 to remove the nest."

"Okay." Whatever. Whatever it took.

I looked around at what I had to eat and drink. A single, open bottle of drinking water I'd left months before was on the counter. That was it. I decided to head out to do some minimal shopping, and get organized for my two-week stay. I was relieved to find the key to the truck. I headed out to the beat-up, long-bed pickup and inserted the key in the ignition and turned. Silence. Complete silence. *Noooooo.* I was so tired and hungry and thirsty and frustrated. And alone. I had been traveling since five that morning. The dead car battery is a frequent issue for snowbirds, unless they have caretakers or renters who keep on top of things. But I had been gone only a few months; the battery shouldn't be dead.

I ran through my options. I could go down the driveway to my neighbors for help, or call someone, but it was already getting late and dark. I decided to go to bed super early with no water or food, or ambient light. I would deal with everything in the morning.

When Honey Man called the next morning for directions, I asked if he could bring jumper cables.

He arrived an hour later with a battery-charging briefcase.

We opened the hood of the truck and connected it to the battery. Nothing happened.

Honey Man looked at the connections, then said, "The charging battery is dead."

He plugged his charger into the temporary electrical meter on the pole in the driveway. "It'll take a while," he said. My eyes followed him as he went back to his truck and took a hit of ganja. Until then, I had not noticed that there were a couple heads in the backseat—a toddler and presumably the toddler's mother.

Honey Man emerged a couple moments later to assess the bee situation.

"I come back in a couple days."

"You can't do it now?"

"No, no. I need my truck and all my equipment." His bee truck was elsewhere. I had come to learn that this is how things work on St. Croix. Tradesmen come to assess, then return to do. Maybe.

"What's your real name, Honey Man?"

"Everyone call me Honey Man."

Once the battery pack was charged, he got the truck up and running. Progress. He would return Friday at dusk when the bees were returning to the hive. It was a lengthy process; he'd need several hours. I was disappointed. I'd hoped to be catching a

sunset somewhere beach side, one of my only pleasures during this construction phase of life on St. Croix.

With the truck purring, I made a run into Christiansted to Twin City Coffee House for a much needed latte, charging the battery as I drove. I was lucky to find a parking place on the side street where government employees park.

After I cut the engine, a sense of dread hit me. I hadn't driven it for twenty minutes. *Let me just check.* I turned the key. Totally silent. My heart sank. The nine-minute drive into town was not enough to recharge the battery, of course.

Already parked, I figured I might as well get a coffee.

When I approached the outdoor patio of Twin City, I looked around. There was a table of brawny guys with DayGlo vests. These guys were all over the island, working for FEMA, WAPA, the refinery, VIYA, the Park Service. Some lived on-island, but most were sent from the continent on a project basis. I ordered my latte and found an empty seat at a nearby table.

I turned to a graying, open-faced man seated nearby and asked softly, nodding my head toward the DayGlo set, "Do you think any of those guys have jumper cables?"

He looked at me, "What, you having trouble with your car?"

I related my conundrum.

He said, "I have cables."

"You do?"

"Yes, but they're at home. I rode my bike here. I need to bike home to get them."

"Oh, no, that's okay. I'm sure someone here has cables."

"It's no trouble," he said. I looked at the slight but able-bodied man, who must have been well into his seventies.

"At least finish your coffee," I said, smiling. I wanted to finish my own. I've met and learned from so many people over coffee at Twin City: the teacher, the young assistant to our Congresswoman, the older elegant couple who owned one of the big shipping businesses, a conservation specialist, a water treatment expert.

"I'm Cynthia," I said.

"Wallace. Wallace Williams." We got chatting. I came to learn that Wallace represented the United States as the first marathon runner from the USVI in the 1988 Seoul Olympic Games and founded The Virgin Islands Pace Runners in 1978. Biking was not a big deal for this lithe, fit gentleman. More: he was the Territory's Librarian, and was a writer, a journalist, often profiling other notables. A year later, the Senate Committee on Culture, Preservation, and Aging recognized him for his many achievements and contributions to the territory.

"I'm done," he said, pushing away from the table. "Where are you parked?"

"Around the corner," I said, pointing. "Long-bed white truck."

"I'll be back in ten minutes," he said.

"Are you sure? I mean—"

"See you soon."

He reappeared fifteen minutes later.

"I couldn't find my cables, but I brought an extra battery."

I popped the hood. He carried over a heavy little metal box. He unhitched and removed the truck's battery and hooked up his own.

"I do want this back, though," he said.

"Of course."

"I'm trusting you," he said. "But this way, you can drive around and get things done, while your battery is being checked out and fixed. Take it to HH."

I was familiar with HH, a quarter mile from 1 Pearl. Anyone who's lived here a minute knows HH. It's where to go for battery and tire issues.

Minutes later, I dropped off the battery and was on my way catching up on my first-day-on-the island errands. Every time I stopped anywhere—the post office, Home Depot, Plaza East—when I got back in the truck and turned the key, it was dead as a doormat. The first time I panicked. But I learned to open the hood and give a little jiggle to the wires connecting the battery, which Wallace had only loosely, temporarily attached. And every time, as soon as I popped the hood, a couple men in the parking lot approached and asked if I needed help. Gotta love St. Croix.

When I circled back to HH, they told me the battery was fully charged, and good to go. They reinstalled it for me—securely—charged me $20 and handed me Wallace's battery.

The next day, I met Wallace in the parking lot near the fort and handed back his battery. I was grateful for his generosity and honored to have made his acquaintance.

For several days I lived on my construction site, giving the swarming nest wide berth. When Honey Man arrived on Friday, he stepped into his beekeeping suit, cutting quite a figure in his getup. He took out a purple box with a dozen empty wood frames. He was so handsome and his gear so elegant, I asked if I could take a picture of him. He smiled broadly as he posed, lying back on the stone wall in front of the flamboyant tree like a Vanna White modeling a new sedan.

He stoked a little fire in a special vessel and then brought it over near the hive to smoke out the bees. Reaching into the stone wall in the belly of the house with his big gloves, he emerged with a handful of bees, hoping the queen was among them. Once the queen was in the box, the rest would follow. He estimated there were eight or nine thousand bees. He offered me a small piece of warm, runny honeycomb. A little dividend. Honey Man owns thousands of hives all over this agricultural island, which he uses to pollinate crops as well as to make honey. He'd take mine out southeast.

Honey Man said he'd been at the house before. The previous owners had offered him the garage roof that they'd torn off.

"They gave you a perfectly good roof? It wasn't the hurricane?"

"There was nothing wrong with it."

The previous owners also had a hive, so he suggested that I close that hole. He left an empty box in case another colony came seeking a place to settle. And they did. A few months later I saw him at the farmers' market where he has a stand with herbs and, of course, honey. I told him the box was full and he came to get it.

That day, that week, I loved St. Croix. All those setbacks forged learning and new connections to people who were warm and helpful and patient, whom I would continue to bump into in unexpected places.

One afternoon months later when I was driving in the rain forest, off the beaten path, among a grove of banana and other trees, I saw Honey Man working among them.

"Hey, Honey Man!"

He looked up and gave me one of his signature smiles.

FRESH IMPRESSIONS

Back. Home. Here.

I've returned. After seven months in my alternate rowing-farm-temperate-Hudson Valley universe, I touch down on tropical St. Croix. There's stasis and change, familiarity and newness, things I expect and surprises, and things I expect but I am still surprised by. Like the heat wave when I exit the small plane and walk across the tarmac. I can never figure out how to dress for JFK's 22 degrees and be ready for the island's 85.

I am gathering impressions, not firsts, as I've been coming here for years. It's not a first but a *fresh* impression—one loaded with relativity, juxtaposed with the Hudson Valley, and the memory—inaccurate or true—I hold of how St. Croix was when I left. I remember this feeling from when I was a young traveler. I returned after months in Latin America to New York City, and was bowled over by fur coats and limousines, normalized by proximity but amplified by distance.

It's there, too, when I have a friend visiting and I experience St. Croix through their eyes, with heightened awareness. Rather than see beyond, I notice the garbage and the flattened buildings. I avert their eyes with mine, make them see what I want them to: the historic architecture in Frederiksted, the curve of the Grand House of Whim Plantation, the mottled blue coastline, the mahoganies lining the road, a Crucian bakery, the goat farm, the most authentic farmstands, its elegant peoples.

I am reintroduced to the melodious, comforting Crucian lilt at the Avis counter, one I've been hearing over the past month as I've planned for reentry. I've spoken to Cliff who has kept an eye on my pool and property, a woman in VIYA customer service and another at Oliver Exterminating. I have more patience and can even find joy with them and their competence and their reassuring voices than I do the offshore customer service variety back in the States with bad connections, stilted English, and who ask me the same questions every time they pass me to someone else. Because they are human, and Crucian and personal.

I drive away in another rental car, gray and non-descript and unassuming as usual, which I never feel comfortable in, but is the cheapest I can find, and one that will serve until I finally find a vehicle I am willing to place a bet on. As the car drives itself out of the airport and toward Christiansted, I take the scenic route up the hill away from Sunny Isle, driving on the left, of course, which feels natural, makes sense to me. I round this bend and the next; it's all coming back. The curves are lodged in my reptilian brain. The same FOR SALE signs are on the side of the road.

Up north, I left a brown field on the verge of winter, dramatic and astounding in its own way, but when I touch down in St. Croix, I am overwhelmed by green. I know, I know: it rained a lot this year, but more. Having left it dry and dusty in March, the greenness is tremendous.

As I round the final bend, things seem a little wild, unkempt, scruffy, in an endearing way, like an adolescent on the day of a haircutting appointment. Vegetation is spilling from the roadside narrowing the passage further, making blind curves even trickier for this out-of-practice island driver. The road crew is likely due here soon. They will wrangle it into submission. But I wonder, were there budget cuts? Is labor scarce? Or has all the rain made it harder to keep up with?

I always felt badly about those who do that brutal work—dressed head to toe like beekeepers in the hot day sun, keeping safe from riled Jack Spaniards and surprised centipedes. The DayGlo cones serve as warning on approach. The weed whacking drones on for hours. After, a guy with a big plastic bag gathers the exposed water bottles, fast-food clams, candy wrappers and tires from the freshly cut grass. I don't love the drone, nor ever thought all that weed whacking necessary until I realized it came with trash pickup, and I grew to appreciate the process more. Today I wonder how long it would take for Rattan Road to disappear without the weed whacking.

As I approach my own modest home, I note, happily, that the half dozen plots of land that were cleared in my neighborhood have grown back, and over. They aren't repopulated with mahoganies and flamboyant as they once were, but at least they're not barren like when I left. This is good news, reassuring. I breathe deeply. Has the real estate surge abated with the pandemic's wane?

Cliff had told me that I lost a flamboyant tree in the driveway, one of those that line the ascent. Thankfully, it is not the one that was bare last year, in a critical place, which miraculously came back to life, and today has a healthy crown. The one that fell won't be missed nearly as much, and it fell away from the driveway into the brush below out of harm's way.

The house is still standing, but I knew that. Looks almost normal. The paint has faded over the past couple years. The frangipani is completely naked, but everything else is exploding. The orchids didn't make it. I won't be seduced this year at the Botanical Garden's orchid table—by Apple or anyone else—to take on an even work-free, completely forgiving orchid.

I don't need to check, but I do, my full cistern. Gratitude.

The pool has a tinge of yellow on the sides. I wonder when Cliff was last here.

On my little hill, it's green in a way that is absent of flowers, but the next day a couple hibiscus pop, and a rash of bougainvillea buds appear. I note the abundant Ginger Thomas, the "national" flower, the following day when I head out east. The yellow bush interspersed with the cacti on the hills creates a visual texture all its own.

My housekeeper came by to open up the house: removed the tarps, vacuumed and

dusted and wiped and cleaned. She did a mammoth job. Though I'll need to re-sponge all the surfaces and I'll do loads of moldy laundry, I know how it would have been had she not come. Last year I arrived after a very long journey, late afternoon, to a house with seven months of centipedes and West African dust. For you full-time islanders, imagine how many critters you encounter in a single day on your floor. Now multiply that by 200. That's what I found in my house last year: Centipedes and gazillions of millipede shells, beetles, and cockroaches, abstracted by time and lifelessness. Saharan dust and local mold everywhere in equal measure.

And every year when I leave, I try to anticipate what might go wrong. I stuff every crevice. I bag and tarp. I take any clothes I care about back to New York. Leftover pressure-treated wood chunks elevate sofas and the dining room table just in case a hurricane hits and there is standing water inside for days. Outdoor furniture comes inside to slow aging, and so a high wind doesn't turn it into torpedoes. I tarp upholstered furniture mostly against mold and dust; I know it will not withstand a hurricane. I've given up on that. There is likely nothing that can be done if the house is directly hit by a hurricane. I take the art off the walls. I unplug lights and appliances and consolidate things into the house's interior. It is not a normal house, and it is not a normal situation.

I close the gate, and let Dexter out of the car. He picks up where we left off. He races around the turnaround, checking on things, and under the house, smells the news, pieces together who's been here. Can he explain the deep hole near the fence that looks like a wild animal (dog?) was trapped and desperately tried to get out, who tore the doormat to pieces and scattered it in the garden?

Dexter hasn't eaten for twenty-four hours and the whole transport is rough on him. He won't eat the food I put out. I need to buy yogurt to mix in. He curls up on my unmade bed as if we've never been gone.

There is potable water in the large five-gallon bottle, which I don't think I'll drink. I hear plastic leaches into the water if it sits too long. Seven months seems like too long. I pour it into the sink to begin cleaning pantry items. As I reach in to wash, something grabs me. I cringe, I gasp. That's when I realize I've been on edge all this time. I fish out a dead centipede, whose pinchers are still at work. I laugh in relief.

Welcome home.

EMBRACING INVASIVES

One morning, as I prepared the guest/Governor's Side of the house for my sister and brother-in-law's arrival, I noticed, in the shadows, a slender triangular-shaped animate object, that could only be construed as a tail, reptilian, with blotched markings, draping down about a foot from the top of the wall. I took a quick photo and backed off, closed the door. I searched online for what it might be with a strong hypothesis: *red-tailed boa constrictor*. I compared my photo with images on the internet. No question it had the same patterns. Boas had become the talk of the town, pervasive and invasive—and creepy—as they were. While boas can bite out of self-defense with their sharp teeth, they are nonvenomous and use constriction to rapidly kill their prey, cutting off the blood supply to vital organs. On Facebook, I found William Coles, the resident boa expert, educator and exterminator. I messaged him asking if he could help me. I received no response.

I went about my day, not too concerned, almost forgetting about the new resident. But when I tucked in at night, it occurred to me, given that the sighting occurred only thirty feet away, through a couple porous walls, I should be dealing with this snake more proactively. Would it come snuggle—tightly— in bed with me in the middle of the night? I lay awake, heart racing, listening to every movement through the door. At midnight, I re-messaged Coles, this time attaching the photo I'd taken. He responded within seconds, asking where I lived, and said he'd be there first thing in the morning.

Coles arrived, as promised. He took out his equipment; I brought over a ladder. I opened the door slowly and pointed. He ascended the ladder without ceremony or trepidation, and from his perch looked down into the wall.

"Just an iguana," he announced. *Phew!* He climbed down from the ladder. "I knew it as soon as I drove up your driveway," he said. "I could hear birds."

At the time, Coles worked for the Division of Fish and Wildlife of the Department of Planning and Natural Resources (DPNR) as the boa exterminator but was being reassigned to teach archery. Why, one wonders, would they move him off the important mission of eliminating the rapidly reproducing, destructive boas? The population was growing exponentially, and they are expanding their territory, moving east. Coles said the snakes preferred the rainforest, and were mostly out west, but they get into the hoods of vehicles parked at Rhythms at Rainbow, say, while the owners enjoy a painkiller or two by the surf, and hitch a ride. He still removes dozens of snakes every year and has a collection of snake skins and jars of meat, which he thought might be an interesting tourist trinket. He talked about recipes. I tuned out.

Like much of the "wildlife" on the island, boas are non-native and without predators. But they've caught the imagination of the residents and end up in a lot of dinner conversations and sometimes dinner itself, like at Ridge to Reef Farm slow-down dinners. I admit that I have yet to eat boa meat, claim to be vegetarian for that course, but friends have tried it, and vouch that it tastes like gamey and muscular and lean—yes— chicken.

Coles packed up and left after about an hour. I was exhausted.

After he left, I realized that the iguana was still in the wall, cohabitating. My urban sister and her husband would be sharing the house with it! I wasn't sure how it got in there, or how to remove it safely. Eventually, a friend who has a pet iguana and likes them, came over to remove it. Many of us on-island are intrigued by but are not in love with iguanas, another invasive species, that can take out a garden in a whipstitch. Some of us

carry a reasonable fear of them, as they can really whack with their tails. One clocked my neighbor's dog in the head, and it was never quite the same. Iguanas are scarce much of the year, but typically start making an appearance in March, when they come out seeking mates. They can be seen crossing the road or up in trees. One (possibly the same one?) comes to visit every year and taunts Dexter from the roof or the mahogany.

None of this concerned my friend. Fearless, she got up on the ladder and peered down into the wall. Nothing there.

*   *   *

In late 2022, DPNR began offering a bounty of $50 for snakes under 4 feet and $100 for those over 4 feet. They trained people in wildlife control, to catch boas, for a nominal fee. According to the *Virgin Island Daily News*, December 3, 2022, many snakes were found in Creque Dam, in the rainforest, but they have also "been found in locations to include dense areas like William's Delight, Estate St. John, Judith's Fancy, and neighborhoods like La Grande Princesse." Grande Princesse, where I live? Uh-oh. I wondered if, and hoped, this was logged because of my false alarm, or whether boas had really made it here, into the little tropical forest outside my window.

The program was so popular and successful that they ran out of funds and had to suspend it in June 2024. There was also an admission that boas would likely never be eliminated on the island; there was no way to keep up. This didn't seem a good reason to stop trying.

The experts disagree about how the boas arrived on St. Croix, but concur that in a decade the number has escalated from one (or several) to tens of thousands—perhaps as many as 80,000. Coles purports that a Hovensa employee had illegal pet snakes and when the refinery closed in 2012, rather than take them home with him, he let them loose. Females can reproduce without males and can give birth to sixty live babies. A single, casual, thoughtless act has led to the decimation of local wildlife and will possibly scare off tourists. Boas prey on mongoose, chickens, dogs, small deer, but the real tragedy is the loss of birds.

As of July 2022, some 267 bird species were recorded in the USVI, according to the *Birds Checklist of the World*. Some birds are native, others migratory, rare, occasional, or introduced. These include many waterbirds, of course: osprey, herons, egrets, pelicans, frigates, spoon-bills, but also birds that live in desert-like ecosystems, grasslands, and rain forests like parakeets and parrots. There are several places for enthusiastic birders to raise their binoculars, such as Sandy Point and Southgate Reserve on the north shore. I've seen kestrels, peregrine falcon, and red-tailed hawks at my place and osprey on the beach. Hummingbirds are regular visitors to the hibiscus and noni. The bananaquit, also known as a sugarbird, is the native "national" bird. And we have peacocks.

Bats are the only native terrestrial mammals on the island, including three fruit eaters (Jamaican fruit-eating bat, Antillean cave bat, and red fig-eating bat), the insectivore velvety free-tailed and Brazilian free-tailed bats, Miller long-tongued bat (which favors cacti) and pescatarian greater bulldog bat. Fruit-eating bats (possibly the red fig-eating?) dropped massive amounts of Pollock-like purple poop all over my pool patio and threw it against the wall one summer when I wasn't here. Thankfully, that happened only once. I power washed and repainted, reupholstered the chaise lounges, and have not seen them

again. I suspect they found a better place to hang out. I see bats swooping around at night, over the pool, and benefit from their voracious appetite for mosquitoes. To be clear, I am appreciative of all the bats on the island, and it is nice to know that St. Croix distinguishes itself in this regard. For those who are fearful, of note, St. Croix doesn't have rabies, and bats provide valuable services. Indeed, the fruit-eating bats play an important role in agriculture. They are responsible for pollinating and dispersing the seeds of important fruits from mangoes to soursop to avocados.

Other than those with wings, most "wildlife" is "exotic." The white-tailed deer were introduced in the 1700s for hunting, and to this untrained eye, look like they have adapted by decreasing in size compared to those I see in New York State. Rats came over in boats centuries ago, the black rat from India and Norway rats from China. In 1884, the small Asian mongoose was brought in to control the rats. Rats are nocturnal, and mongoose are diurnal, so the planned predation didn't pan out. Plus, the rats got clever. They learned to live in the treetops (they are known for making nests in palm trees) to avoid the mongoose. Instead of helping with the rats, the mongoose population went through the roof and ended up driving the endemic St. Croix racer snake to extinction and extirpated the St. Croix ground lizard from the main island of St. Croix, according to the *Exotic Invasive Species, US Virgin Islands Facts Sheet, 2012*.

And invasives are not just the fauna, of course. The tan-tan, or guinea tamarind, from Central America, and coral vine from Mexico are two of many invasive species of flora that have spread like wildfire. Aggressive growers with strategies that conquer, they both take over open, sunny spots and crowd out native species. The coral vine blankets entire roadsides and forest edges, smothering anything in its path.

So, now, the boas are taking care of the mongoose. I do feel like I have seen fewer mongoose than when I first arrived a few years back, but that may just be the power of suggestion at work. I am not feeling great about the boas, in general, but if they knock out some mongoose, I'm okay with that. Better them than the birds and bats.

NEIGHBORHOOD LAUNDRY

I drive by NEIGHBORHOOD LAUNDRY daily on my way to other things. Today, President's Day, underwear is running low, and dirty clothes pile high. I note when I pass there are only a few cars in the lot—a good time to get clean. So on a perfect beach day at high noon, despite the call of the turquoise Caribbean water, I load an overflowing plastic basket into my sandy truck and circle back. I'll spend the afternoon in a high-ceilinged metal shack with sweeping fans and wide-open doors.

The laundromat is an anonymous, serious place where women get the job done. The intimacy of our wares and cataloguing of personal items perhaps demands privacy, a certain disinterest. Some juggle multiple loads of laundry and children. A couple girls assist, for fun or because of clear expectations. I ponder how the perfectly-folded, colorful pairs of small pantie columns stay that way in the bureau, why it's worth the trouble.

It's not as hot as you'd think under the fans.

NEIGHBORHOOD LAUNDRY refers to location rather than personality. People are not unfriendly, but it is not *neighborhoodly*. Indeed, there's a hint of competition, driven by efficiencies and preferencess for washers, dryers, bins and folding surfaces. Irritation hangs in the air, too, as bored children tug their mothers' leggings. One toddler insists on pushing a cart to her grandmother's annoyance.

"I'm too old for this," she says, grabbing the girl. There's resignation, too.

It'd been a while since I'd done laundry in a communal laundromat. I've washed my clothes in apartment building basements and my own home. But here, on St. Croix, I decided to delay purchase of a washer and dryer until construction was complete, when I returned the following winter. On an island where brine takes a toll, metal is vulnerable and rodents run rampant, appliances age prematurely. Besides, water is precious and electricity expensive; the laundromat offers value. I could drop off my laundry, pay a little extra to save scarce time. But I've chosen to do it myself for reasons beyond time and money. I'm keeping it real. That's what I'm doing. And I'm proud, even a tad smug, that I am shoulder-to-shoulder folding sheets with the neighboring neighborhood of Sion Farm at NEIGHBORHOOD LAUNDRY.

I'm an irregular regular. I've never seen another white person. A rarity, like the men, I am not *other*. No one treats me as an outsider. My newness defines me more than my whiteness. I don't have the process down like the experienced. Women help and include me, in subtle ways, asking if they can have my washer when I'm done, or tell me *that dryer's not working*. I'm learning. I know now to claim a rolling bin on arrival, preferably one with a hanging rack, easier to push than one without. The rack comes in handy, too, to air dry items. Others bring hangers for their delicates; I may do the same next time, if I remember.

There's a washing machine hierarchy: large and newer—and working. Some have been inoperable for months. I've learned that if there's a nice-looking empty washer, it's likely not functioning. I've learned to check for tape across the coin slot before committing with clothes and detergent. Once assessed, I load the clothes, with a casual nod to separating colors. I lift the heavy rubbery flap, pour detergent into the left chute, crank the front door closed. I head for the change machine. A handwritten note says *out of order.* I flag the busy manager who retrieves a shoe box from the office. I give her a twenty-dollar bill; she hands me two rolls.

I insert quarters into the slot, trusting the digital screen's count-down. At $2.75, it stops. I've shoved quarters too fast. I push the button, smack the washer. Quarters reappear. I insert them, again, more slowly, turning Washington the other way. The screen freezes.

"Machine's jammed," I say to the woman, who nods to a guy who comes over to unlock the machine top and rummages inside and finds my quarters. He pushes them into the slot one by one with patience I don't have. He smiles.

I'm learning to slow down.

When the machines are swishing and spinning, I sit on the stoop beside a girl who twirls her pencil above a workbook and then dive-writes with enthusiasm, like a pelican after a fish. The laundromat is across from the elementary school where, during the week, uniformed children play in the yard in the hot sun. A couple times I've seen a girl among the boys on the basketball court. I slowed to watch her drive to the basket. When she missed and fell on the tarmac, the boys laughed and whooped. I wanted to give her a pep talk and give them a scolding. But she got up and she was there the next time I passed. I wonder where she gets the strength, the confidence. I can empathize with her desire to play. In another world, decades ago, I was that girl.

A man stacks dark blue jeans and white tees. He must separate them to keep them unadulterated. His presence reminds me how few men come here.

Children clamber and perch on the only bench near the flat-screened TV in poses adults don't strike, holding their own small screens. The TV's running the news, but without sound it's just backdrop.

Sand on the bottom of the laundry basket reminds me where I'll be at sunset.

PRINTOUT

On a bright February day, I sit in a tidy, air-conditioned, L-shaped, shades-of-white tiled room in a strip mall in Sion Farm down the road from where I live. I pass the cheery, text-packed, blue-and-orange sign, at least twice a day: *We are your one stop Printing and Document Center that caters to ALL your printing needs...!* Thirty-five kinds of printing are listed including key chains and placemats and laminating. Number one on the list is T-Shirt Printing, followed by Funeral Booklets.

Inside, a lone, albeit capable and poised, woman mans a couple desktop computers and a printer. A half dozen tee-shirts of varying sizes and colors hang on the wall, along with colorful pieces of paper that say, "I am 5 by 7," "I am 8 by 11."

I forwarded an email with an attachment, a contract I need to print and sign, to the House of Printing and am waiting for it to come through so the young woman can print it. Someone in my writing group—actually, several—said it was easy to get things printed, insisted I do it, so I can hand out copies of my stories at the Writer's Circle on Mondays. I'm giving printing a whirl with this single-pager. So far it is not going well.

The calm young woman is juggling my demands with those of a fatigued-looking woman who sits near the door, with small wire glasses and snug jeans. She was here before me, holding on her lap a young girl who is darker than herself and a perfect little package of unblemished caramel skin, compact miniature person-body, pierced ears, large, curious eyes. When the little girl squirms, trying to escape her perch, the woman, who seems a tad old to have a girl that age, tells her to stop with firm but not unkind intolerance. The girl puts her ring and middle fingers into her mouth and sucks, looking directly at me, the braids on her head creating something of a question mark. I try a smile; she looks at the floor. I can't imagine what harm would come from allowing the girl to roam the room, but the woman is clear; she wants her to be still.

I have been waiting ten, fifteen minutes, which isn't a long time in the scheme of things, but for something that takes ten, fifteen seconds back in New York, where I own a printer, it seems like a lot, especially because it was a drive-by decision. I was on my way to the bank, Home Depot and Peter's Rest Convenience Center, aka the dump, when I thought, *okay*.

The wall of windows reveals the sun continues to bake my truck outside. I need to get going. I'm not sure this one page is worth the wait but have no idea where and how else I can get the printing done, and I need to do it.

"Large," the woman says, when the young woman points at the tee shirt sizes.

She has chosen bright yellow and red.

I see a photograph of a man with a crown on his head, several lines of text, but cannot make out more than *King*.

"Did you get a return-receipt?" the calm, multitasking young woman asks. It takes a moment for me to realize she is directing the question at me.

"No, not yet," I say, checking my phone again.

"It gives an automatic return-receipt when we receive it."

A minute or two later, I see a MAILER-DAEMON message. I missed a letter in the address. Argh. I try forwarding the contract again, this time doublechecking the address on the business card she handed me earlier.

I contemplate the handsome taupe-colored tee; they aren't bad shapes and quality for the price. I should print a few with my artwork or a photo of Dexter.

A few minutes later, I get an automatic receipt.

"Got it," I call over to the young woman now retrieving the other woman's project in the back room.

"Okay," she throws over her shoulder.

I look over to the seated woman. "You are printing tee shirts? What's the occasion?" thinking there must be a wedding, a store opening, a birthday, thinking I could share in her celebration, the excitement, for a brief moment.

The woman looks at me without expression through her small, cloudy glasses. "My son was killed."

"Oh . . . I'm so sorry."

"Right here." She waves a finger towards the window. "Car accident."

"That's terrible."

"Very early in the morning."

"People drive so crazy."

"They were arrested."

"What a tragedy. I can't imagine."

I am stunned.

I am curious by nature, but sometimes my questions take me to places maybe I shouldn't go. I don't see whether the little girl is still squirming or still, the little girl who likely lost her father. The woman, presumably her grandmother, will honor her father by wearing his likeness, his love-ness, over her heart.

A few days later I will pass the entrance to the mall's parking lot and on the side of the road see a commemorative white cross and a beige poster that looks like the tee shirt, ornamented with white and red and yellow flowers. Drive Safely/In Memory of. . . Eggie. Right there. I hadn't seen it before, right in front of the printing store. I will take a picture, and then spend time online looking for Davindra Ramsundar, "Eggie," who died November 3rd, at 5:00 am, at age 24, whose grieving family and friends fought for justice when the offending surviving speeder had inconsistent explanations about what happened that morning in the wee hours. A video recorded Eggie signaling to make a right-hand turn, and the other car ran into him on his right. Eggie sustained fatal injuries to his upper torso. I will find that he graduated salutatorian from his high school and attended UVI and was God-fearing. And while he was survived by a girlfriend, there is no evidence of a daughter. But I think this sweet girl is the one in a video on his Facebook page dancing in his honor, although the video is from the back, and she looks a little pudgier.

A friend who has lived on St. Croix for decades says that everyone has lost a young man on this island tourists call Paradise, this island whipped by hurricanes and grief.

I think about how we mourn in different ways.

I think about how people are resigned, tolerant, give into death. How they have no choice.

I think about the quote on the poster, from Revelation 21:4: "And God will wipe away every tear from their eyes; there shall be no more death, nor sorrow, nor crying."

I think about how one of St. Croix's many charms —along with saying *Good Day* when you walk into a room full of strangers—is the unique driving etiquette. A driver on the main road will stop, flash headlights, hold up traffic, to let a person out of a side road, or take a turn in front of them, and not only when they are turning in. The gesture is polite and thoughtful but also underscores the patience of island culture. Generosity, not urgency, is the organizing framework. It occurs to me that the stopping makes things safer, too; it slows down everyone so those turning are less likely to get sideswiped. I haven't articulated this before with Crucians to understand their motivations or confirm how they think about this. They likely don't think about it at all. It is just the way they are, who they are. Kind.

But all that is irrelevant when it comes to the random, insane drivers who defy all sense of decorum, drive at ridiculous speeds in the middle of the night or cross the middle line around blind curves, race each other down the highway, those likely under the influence and who slam into the sons of God-fearing women like the one in this room.

The young woman nods us both over to the cashier. The tee shirts are bagged. The woman and young girl leave.

My single page printout lies on the counter.

"How much?"

"Twenty-five cents."

I write and sign my name. "Could you make a copy, please?" I find two quarters. "Do you sell envelopes?" I ask.

She fingers through a cabinet and finds one. "Thirty-five cents."

"That's fine. Thanks." I give her two more quarters.

They take care of all your printing needs. All of them. But I think I'll be buying myself a printer soon.

A BREEZY AFFAIR

Things did not start off well. Our relationship was rocky at best.

When I purchased my ruin of a house on St. Croix, broken concrete block surrounded the structure and filled the garden beds. Shards had been hurled over the stone wall into the bush. Piles and piles. Whole mountain ranges. On closer inspection, I learned these were not the remnants of ordinary concrete block, but *decorative* or *architectural* or *breeze* block. Once painted white, they were shattered beyond their original definition. The previous owners had knocked them out of their openings, from walls, with considerable hostility and determination. I could feel their dejection and rejection, their shame, and I adopted a loathing for these faceless fragments that were everywhere they shouldn't be.

My prejudice, like all prejudices, was based on ignorance and fear— and the onerous, backbreaking work they represented.

When I finally decided to be rid of them, I filled two large white plastic paint buckets weighing fifty pounds and lugged them up a flight of brick stairs over the patio, up three more, through the breezeway to the driveway where I loaded them onto the pickup. Dozens of times. I did it myself because I thought the work was too demeaning to hire someone else to do. I drove load after load to Peter's Rest Convenience Center in buckets and contractor bags in my rattling, arthritic, long-bed pickup, and heaved them into the dumpster.

Even then, I wasn't completely done with them. A couple of walls still had decorative block on what would become the kitchen, and on the other end of the house in the laundry room. A garden partition contains a slender one-block-wide stack. These remained. They survived the sledgehammer of the previous owners. I didn't love them. I thought them tired and tacky but kept them as a nod to the house's origins. And I wasn't sure what to do with those walls and openings. Replace them with windows? Close them up and make a solid wall?

But they still puzzle me. These blocks are part of two exterior walls separating the outdoors, and daunting night, from the inside. Pictures of the house from decades ago show the large window openings filled with breeze blocks. This is the part I don't understand: while they create a wall, they allow the passage of West African dust, mosquitoes, and vermin. When I've asked Crucians, and people who have lived on-island forever, they never gave a thought to breeze blocks. They tell me that West Indians don't care about mosquitoes, and dogs "handle" the rodents that might squeeze through. On the kitchen wall, I saw the vestiges of where a screen might have been tacked on the inside and took a cue from it. We installed tailor-made screens on the outside of the house in those two spots.

Stepping back to research and observe how architectural block is used on other houses, I began to realize they are an apt solution for a myriad of issues, and I've developed an appreciation for them. A sturdier alternative to a metal or wood fence, breeze blocks won't rust in the sea air, be eaten by termites, or blow over in a hurricane. They require little upkeep. The breeze block provides shade and a privacy screen in high density neighborhoods, retains a dog, withstands high winds, while letting a breeze through. Indeed, I've noticed the breeze block wall in my kitchen condenses and channels the passage of air to augment it in a pleasant way, like a gentle, multi-faceted wind tunnel. Hence, *breeze block*? I've been told it is good to have an opening at the back of the house, for a hurricane wind as a relief valve, so the roof doesn't blow. Although that raises another question: what is the back when the wind is moving in circles?

On St. Croix, as elsewhere, I imagine, these patterned blocks show up mostly in yard walls or patios, with a good deal of fanfare and often with an energetic or possibly jarring combination of color. Orange and white is a popular pairing. This Caribbean interpretation can be charming in its own way but installed with restraint and an architectural eye, breeze blocks can inject visual interest in an otherwise mundane wall, define an interior courtyard, or demarcate (and hide) a parking area. When I studied a couple homes closely recently, I came to understand their midcentury origins and appeal. When breeze blocks share the color or hue of the house, or have a natural ceramic tone, they can be modern, stylish, even beguiling.

Once I started looking and seeing, and as I travel the island, I note there are many variations of decorative blocks, likely demarcating different eras or manufacturers. Houses might be datable by their block design. Circles, stars, suns, flowers, pinched, square, linear, geometric. Stacking and aligning is often required to complete their designs. But I am concerned for my recent infatuation. I don't see new structures integrating breeze blocks. At my usual home improvement centers—where I've spent many hours over the years— I saw no decorative block for sale, only basic concrete block with two or three holes (which can also create a breezy wall if laid on their side). A friend told me he found a stash on the west end, but I wonder if they are still being made and sold. I suspect they will be making a comeback with the revival of mid-century architecture and stronger weather. My prediction: we will be seeing more of them, embracing them, and catching a gentle breeze.

HOUSES OF ST. CROIX

You could say I stalk houses. There are houses which cry for attention and quiet ones I seek out and slow for. Despite the walls and fences, I have trespassed only from the road and yet I do wonder if my slowing down, my observing, is wrong in some way, invasive, voyeuristic. Is the natural way to see a house at forty miles an hour? Would it be less intrusive if I were on foot? Perhaps it feels awkward because the houses I relish are for the most part modest dwellings, not asking for attention. I have thought about creating a photo-infused coffee table book of these and other noteworthy St. Croix houses, with blurbs on their owners and their stories, but am not sure how it would be received. So I have tried to use words to create the images. Even so, have I committed a form of inadvertent appropriation, or is it appreciation, as I hope?

I hurtle my way down to Ha' Penny beach most days with my dog Dexter in the backseat for his salty, sandy, ocean walk. Along the way, one such house is a quarter mile south of the Synagogue: a lemon-yellow, large, flat, rectangular structure, set back. A tall chain-link fence runs along the road, with three indents where a car can pull in to open or close the gates that swing from two columns crowned by beehive lamps. The patio runs the length of the house and is outlined by bulbous, curvaceous concrete columns topped with additional white metalwork, in a pattern of bricks laid vertically. Intricate, lacy lattice is woven on the windows within. The overall effect is complex; layers of geometric shapes compete for the eye's focus. The seafoam colored roof edge has angled supports that lean away from the body of the house, triangulating, wing-like on the ends, Asian in feel. Despite being held hostage to its metal encasement, the house looks a little like a UFO, as if it might lift off, if it could shake all its strictures. This house serves as a warning, a reminder, that for security reasons, as we discourage trespassers and ward off danger, many of us on St. Croix live in glorified cages, behind bars. I am amused that even though the house and property is consumed in fencing, and screams KEEP OUT, the dark crimson metal gates are usually open when I pass.

Two bends down from this house, after passing three churches in rapid succession, on one of those 90-degree turn non-corners, are two rare wooden dwellings, across the road from one another. They have similarities, but the one on the eastern side, set back and below road grade, draws me in. At its corners, crumbling concrete footings hoist the simple wood-frame box off the ground so it visually floats, which anywhere is remarkable, but here, where most structures are concrete and built atop cisterns and secured to the land, this is an outlier. Once painted pale yellow, the siding has been in large part stripped by weather or hand to reveal dark brown, possibly mahogany wood. A white porch on the corner facing the road is cut into the rectangular prism. Concrete stairs rise to the porch and front door, blocked by a round black object. The rusty corrugated roof, interrupted by rips and curls, ends

with the walls. The siding and roof are in rougher shape as it moves away from the road. The whole house slopes and leans at its underbelly joints. Windows are louvre, curtained and mostly shut, as are the couple shuttered wooden vents. I have never seen anyone near this distinctive, humble dwelling, although the lawn is putting-green short. It has a single shorn bush in front near the patio and a tree on its northern side. Its down-to-earth profile, materials, and lack of bars, makes it seem at once comfortable with and vulnerable to the elements, trespassers, and critters. In contrast to the UFO, this house is exposed—on all sides, from all directions, even below. I wonder how it withstood the hurricanes over the centuries and was not carried away. My friend, Lenny James, a Crucian, informed me that these homes are called "superficiary houses." On Contract Day, the houses were moved to where the enslaved would next be working. Ah so.

A few hundred feet later, a sand-colored geodesic dome swells on the left. I've never been a fan of these space-age structures, despite my admiration for the idea of them and their creator, Buckminster Fuller. They seem out of place wherever they bump up. But perhaps here such a structure makes sense: the design offers unparalleled strength, and its roundish contour likely encourages hurricane winds to pass around and over it with ease, caressing its flanks. On this one, the dome is interrupted by a pair of hexagonal windows and a cupola on its apex. It has an entrance, and three other antithetical "normal" windows every quarter, and its lines are softened by plantings. There's a bright pool out back, along with a handful of vehicles crowded into the bush. I was once told, when I considered erecting a silo to accompany my barn in the Hudson Valley, that people go crazy living in round spaces, that humans need rectilinearity. I am not convinced this is true, but I do wonder how shelves and bureaus and beds fit efficiently into a limited circular structure. This dome gets me thinking about all that and who decided to put one up on St. Croix, and whether they held onto their sanity.

On the way home from the beach, I take a different route, by Cane Garden Plantation then Plaza East. I wind through Estate Sion Farm, demarcated by its welcoming blue trunks, a dense collection of chunky concrete homes with their own look both collectively and individually. Their upper torsos cantilever a few feet out above their narrower bases, elevating them in a step function, with a certain rhythm and geometry. I assume they are built atop cisterns but am not sure when I follow the rooflines and look for signs of water catchment. The flat overhanging roofs, boxy countenance, vigorous use of breeze blocks, and mostly wider louvre windows, sometimes decorated with small panes, create a mid-century modern look; indeed, this neighborhood was built in the sixties. No-nonsense concrete, sturdy, hurricane-proof construction is obfuscated with decorative block and playful colors, as if neighbors compete for or at a minimum seek distinction: plum, orange, pea green, mustard, turquoise, ruby, teal. Given the way addresses on the island work, I can imagine it is easier for visitors to say, *the purple house following the orange one*. I have explored some of the side streets on occasion and am forced to do so when the nearby school gets out and traffic is redirected, but I am most familiar with the houses along the road opposite the jarring blue Sion Farm Distillery and then, after the turn, across from the sun-drenched, jubilant school. There's a lot to take in, what with all the colors and elaborate wall-fences. Roosters crow. Thick protective aluminum foil fills the windshields of cars parked on the street. Dusty dogs on chains bark, and sleeping ones bake in concrete driveways.

    One house in particular catches my attention; I try to decipher what's going on. Its bright orange contrasts with layers and layers of bold yet intricate white fencing, on the wall by the road, on the patio, and deep-set windows beyond. The grating creates a busy network of lines, like the UFO house, but given its proximity to the road, allows for closer inspection. Christmas palms shade the entrance, and potted plants crowd the front yard.

    There is something about the little development I find charming, possibly the nod to mid-century lines, but when I mentioned this to a friend who grew up on St. Croix, she corrected me, saying that the houses were abysmal, hot and without ventilation. I was shaken to hear this; there seems to be so much life and pride and character and community.

    I pass NEIGHBORHOOD LAUNDRY and the black plastic possibly organic farm

on the left, and a ferocious rat-bat dog who charges me as I drive by, who I confirm and am amazed to see is still alive each day, until I don't. A few hundred feet beyond, there is a small, raised forest-green cinder block house with clean lines and a subdued palette. A handsome black deck and stairs at the front lead to a white door. It is situated back from the road up a small incline, with a narrow Norfolk pine towering three times as tall on the left and a generous, round, shiny breadfruit tree on the right, lending scale, textural contrast, and considerable style. When I stopped to take a photo last week, a muscular short-haired black dog shot out and a large pickup truck sat in the yard; both seemed incongruous with this quiet dwelling. A couple days later, a silver vintage convertible crouched in the shade, which somehow seemed more appropriate.

Next door, a gracious, light blue-green, mid-century single-story home nestles into the same slope, with a large, leaning, sculptural flamboyant, close-cropped frangipani, a banana tree, and a short palm against the wall. The front has decorated breeze block painted in the same powdery green, interrupted by a narrow gate with thoughtfully-designed wrought iron, opening into a small courtyard beyond. The defining edge of the almost flat roof is painted dark green. This gentle house seems to have an interior life and a sense of self and place and elegance.

I look into these houses. I pause. I document them in my head. I do not know the occupants, but I ponder, gather clues, search for signs of life. I am often surprised. Occasionally, I see a car enter the driveway, a person in the door, and I feel like I may know a little about them and update my "records." When I try to catalogue these houses when I'm home, I realize I haven't seen them well enough, so when I pass them again, I stop and take mental note, and sometimes photos. How did I miss the patio when it's so obvious? Or the dark green roof line? I'm amazed what I miss after I've seen each hundreds of times, even studied them intently.

While I'm slowing again, making my rounds, I hear a TED talk on NPR on memory, how we have trouble remembering because we don't pay attention or capture a specific detail to begin with, unless there's meaning, impact, emotion. It's a little like that video, the "selective attention test," where the viewer is asked to count how many passes of a basketball have been made by a half dozen people; the viewer doesn't notice a gorilla that walks right through the scene. Selective attention. Selective memory. And so it was with the black deck on the front of that one house. I never saw that until I took a photo, even though it is right there, as they say, hiding in plain sight, even though I made special note of the colors of the windows and front door.

It reminds me how eyewitnesses must get things wrong, a lot.

These are not houses which make magazine covers or will be featured in real estate listings. They are authentic, modest, maybe vacant, yet intriguing. There are many grander or historic houses on the island, but these possess and are grounded by a certain energy, a presence. They are familiar friends which accompany me daily. They were there for me when I was trying to figure out the ruins of my own house, how to deal with the island's amalgam of challenges: hurricanes, security, color, landscaping, fencing, and materials that withstand the briny breeze. I learn a little something every time I drive by, slowly.

IN LINE AT WAPA

On account of COVID, the Department of Planning and Natural Resources (DPNR, which serves as the building department, among other things) office was open to the public only on Tuesday and Friday. On Tuesday mid-afternoon, I received a call that my Certificate of Occupancy and Electrical Certificate were ready. There was not enough time to go that afternoon and make it before closing, so Friday, I drove an hour round trip west to Frederiksted. I wanted to retrieve the papers as soon as possible, certainly before they were misplaced, or DPNR changed their mind—not that either would happen. Mostly I wanted to check an item off the to-do list, move the ball forward.

I entered the air-conditioned, empty lobby. An unmasked woman came to front office, behind Plexiglas.

"Good morning. I'm here to pick up my C of O . . . Cynthia McVay?"

"Oh, yes."

She went to the back office, returned with two sheets of paper and placed them in a purple folder which she slipped beneath the window.

"No fee."

"So, I'm done? This is it? You don't need to see me again?" I smiled. I sought confirmation that my big project and little house which I scrapped together in an unconventional way has, in fact, passed.

"Yes, unless you want to do something else. Then you come back."

"Thank you. Thank you for all your help." I recognized the name on her name tag. She wrote me from her personal email a few times, shepherding me through the process, since the office was closed, my phone was not working, and the electrical inspector was unable to reach me. I know more about her than I should because I looked her up, found her on Facebook, to make sure I spelled her name correctly in the email since I had a hard time making it out over the phone.

As much as it commemorated and concluded a two-year relationship, the DPNR visit was quick, painless, uneventful.

On my way out the door, she said, "Take that down to WAPA."

"Yes, thank you."

"The one in Sunny Isle."

"Yes, thanks."

I drove the folder twenty minutes back east, a couple miles from my house. I secured it under my phone and mask on the passenger seat, so it didn't waft out the open window as I rolled down Centerline Road.

Water and Power Authority (WAPA) is our unpopular utilities provider. Frequent outages, cumbersome bureaucracy and high cost have made it the laughingstock and source of outrage on St. Croix for locals and recent settlers alike. I hadn't encountered any significant issues yet, and my electric bill stayed under $100 per month for five years, although it took two years for them to remove a pole in my driveway after we had agreed it was unsafe, unnecessary and unsightly. I rerouted the wires so they didn't hang overhead off that pole leaning towards the house. After months and dozens of calls, I eventually convinced a road crew to spontaneously come up with their specialized crane and flatbed to remove it.

WAPA is housed in a nondescript beige-yellow building opposite the mostly empty Kmart across from the mostly empty parking lot of yet another strip mall and asphalt scab, a distinctly American architectural contribution. I park and lock my little blue Kia rental directly in front of WAPA.

Signs all over the window scream, compete for attention.

NO MASK NO SERVICE.

IN OBSERVANCE OF MARTIN LUTHER KING DAY WE WILL BE CLOSED ON MONDAY.

I am not happy about going to WAPA on a Friday afternoon, especially before a three-day weekend. I assess the situation. Two service windows, and a third, fifty feet off to the right. A long line stretches on a shaded porch, a line extended by six-foot markers, like for a track meet, dictating COVID distances. How many people are already there, wrapping around the corner? A dozen? It's either today or another time. I'm here.

I ask a woman with small glasses standing near the front, "Is this customer service?" It's important to know what line is what before you spend an hour standing in it.

"Yea. This is customer service. Cashier's down there."

I take my place behind a petite, trim woman half my size who stands quietly, her dark hair pulled back, her jeans and face pressed, hands folded in front of her. Just as I do, a laborer, with a mask on his chin and baggy shorts and a white tee, takes his place next in line behind me. He talks at large and then finds an audience in a woman in the blue scrubs of a healthcare worker who arrives just after him. Before long, she removes her mask, too, talking to that guy. I turn away, angling my body so if there were a breeze—there isn't—respiratory droplets won't float toward me. But I am getting close to the garbage can. My blood pressure is ratcheting up. It is the early days of COVID, and everything, everywhere is terrifying.

No one will say anything to them, even though there are signs all over the place, and they are putting us at risk. I try to calm myself: Although I'm closest, risk is still minimal. We are outside and I am standing at the far end of my mark on a hypotenuse.

A couple weeks ago I was in line in the Post Office. The militaristic woman behind the glass (the Post Mistress?) kept people true to the rules within the service window area. A second line for packages, beyond her visual jurisdiction, developed. She came out occasionally to keep people in line, which I appreciated. We stood behind our six-foot markers with our masks on as time marched on. Two young teen boys entered. One wore a mask, the other did not. He didn't even have one hanging on his ears, gripping his chin. As they stood there, the mask-wearer moved his down to his chin, so it no longer covered his mouth or nose. We were inside, not outside. Their being white, and everyone in line but me being a person of color, seemed to me to be an assertion of white privilege, young as they were, among older people with greater risk. The one without a mask was red in the face, nervous or excited, possibly because he knew he was breaking the rules. He made no eye contact with anyone as he shoved his hands into his pockets and looked through the glass doors beyond.

No one said anything, but I felt personally responsible for those two white boys' behavior. After a spell of them standing in defiance of the basic rules and minimal courtesy, I burst.

"Put your masks on or go outside."

The woman beside me turned and said, "They are supposed to be wearing masks."

Of course they were supposed to be wearing masks. There were signs all over the place. We were ten months into COVID, pre-vaccine.

Emboldened, I said, "Both of you, go outside!" And they did.

Ten minutes later, a thick-necked man, clad in a red-white-and-blue shirt with stripes and stars emerged from the inner sanctum with something— an x-box? The red-faced boy approached him—his father? — his face a siren. They turned and got into their souped-up Wrangler just outside the entrance.

At WAPA, I was the only white person in line. I was not responsible for the guy behind me, or the healthcare worker who should know better and be a role model. I wouldn't say anything, although I almost have a physical need. I had no right to make a fuss, to enforce rules among this group. Everyone stared straight ahead. Where do they get their calm? Maybe I need a god. I took a deep breath.

I looked across the parking lot at the Kmart. I'd come to know it relatively recently; we were on a first-name basis. Its full name is, in block print: KMART KENMORE CRAFTSMAN SEARS on its yellowish block exterior. When another merger occurred, someone hoisted a ladder, and more letters went up. Kmart is another retailer hanging on for dear life; I have never seen more than a couple cars parked in front. This outpost was a reminder of the failed retailers of the 20th century, an amalgamation, what's left after retail elsewhere has moved on and is reinvented, the remnants of an era, a distillation of franchises and distributors breathing their last breath on an island where appliance options are few. Everyone blames Amazon for brick-and-mortar's demise, and then COVID, but SEARS died a slow death over half a century, afloat only because of its Latin American presence.

Kmart was mismanaged, a scramble, from the get-go. I remember in the 1990's looking for laundry detergent at a Kmart in New Jersey. I finally found it in the lemon-scented area, with dishwasher soap and other cleansers, organized not by function or even brand but by *scent*. It was a mess. Before moving to St. Croix, I had entered a Kmart only once in my life, but here on-island I became a regular, that is, before I discovered COST U LESS, which I resisted at first, enjoying the sense of discovery and Middle Eastern bent at the bazaar-like Plaza East.

I worked in retail for years as a consultant and as VP for a large international retailer which was the largest mall lessee in the U.S. when malls were all the rage. We had a dozen stores in almost every mall in the country. I follow the industry now informally from the sidelines, or, in this case, from across the parking lot. I never liked the smell or texture of malls, so was not cut out for the requisite weekend mall visits expected of senior management. I am encouraged that the monolithic inauthentic structures that overtook suburbs all over the country by the thousands, draining main streets, are finding new purpose as healthcare providers, distribution centers and retirement communities.

Anyway, I knew this Kmart well—we have memories, a certain amount of intimacy and vulnerability—since I finally broke down and bought a washer and dryer there in December, spending double what I'd hoped. Pathetic SEARS KENMORE CRAFTSMAN KMART had me by the appliance balls because shipments may or may not arrive at Home Depot on Tuesday or Wednesday or some other day. Expectations were adjusted weekly by drive-by drop-ins. I got to know all the Home Depot appliance people by name, personally, as they did me. The only way to get what you really want is to place a special order and then wait months for its arrival and not be able to pursue other more immediate options. What does arrive at Home Depot seems to be at the whim and discretion of a distant distribution center, shipping and customs agents, vulnerable to weather and shipping conditions. Would it arrive before I left for the season? I decided to buy something that was right in front of me.

So, it is here at the Kmart, a cool place to go on a hot afternoon, that I found a matching Kenmore brand washer and dryer, committed to them wondering how long Kenmore will be around for warranty and parts purposes after I forked over several grand. My purchase likely covered the saleswoman's salary and rent (what could that be on the island?) for another month. I paid double what I wanted to pay but was told I could get a 40% rebate at the Department of Energy (around the corner from DPNR—a half hour away) because they were ENERGY SAVER. I traveled three times with the forms and receipts and ID, and so spent hours trying to extract thousands of rebate dollars, but the hostile woman who was in charge of the rebate program (and told me I should enjoy the drive—she did!) found one hoop to jump through after another for me, each time different. The final one (which was not mentioned at the start, and certainly not by the Kmart salesperson) was that I had to be a permanent resident to get the rebate. I never got my rebate and wasted a lot of energy in the process.

I have done a half dozen loads of laundry since my purchase. On my own little amortization schedule, I'm down to $300 a load.

One day Kmart will shutter when someone back at HQ doesn't want to print out the USVI page anymore, or watch for hurricanes, or answer any more questions about when the market will pick up for $2000 appliances—when people are lined up across the street trying to keep their power on—or the lease is up, or when it costs less to close the store than to keep it running, when inventory is no longer replenished, or has cash flow issues, or Home Depot gets their act together. Or all of the above.

Thirty minutes into my WAPA wait, a tall woman with an informal, open nature arrived. She chatted to the healthcare worker, moved to a place behind, cracked a joke, and then joined the woman I initially queried at the front of the line. She was loud, nasally and demonstrative, slightly entertaining but she had essentially cut in line, endearing herself to others as she did. She approached the window, the first of many times, while others were already there, and in between. When an older woman was saying with sadness, with resignation, *I won't have power for a week?*, Loudmouth shouldered in, her mask on her chin, I'm pretty sure, not on behalf of the older woman but on behalf of herself.

The line had not moved much but had grown behind me. I advanced one demarcation, around the corner, closer to the garbage can. It rained briefly.

I came armed with a book—I always travel with reading material—having foreseen this wait, this line, my impatience, so I pulled it out and tried to read, to quell, to blot out my annoyance, the heat, the line, the power that WAPA has over us, the incompetence, butting Loudmouth. I read, and I also found that my phone worked, for some reason, maybe because we were so close to VIYA, so I caught up on news and emails. It was not all a waste, but I am not good with waiting. It is not my forte. Driven by productivity, results, efficiencies, beauty, waiting in line, in a parking lot, is very hard for me. I am my worst self when I waste time.

We, dutiful, obedient line makers observed quietly for an hour as Loudmouth went to the window a half dozen times removing her mask to hurl her words and microscopic spit at the Plexiglas. She was not helping The Situation. She was no longer endearing but seemed to be friends or in cahoots with the woman at the front who was still there after an hour.

I overheard the plight of others in the WAPA line. Half the people—mostly women—did not have electricity and discovered it's because there was an outstanding bill, so they could have gone directly to the payment window, but they seemed to have been caught unawares. Another group, often the younger women, seemed to be moving or making adjustments to their living arrangements and needed leases and IDs and to fill out forms to prove these changes—it never seemed to be enough, a little like with the rebates. They went back to the window, the line, multiple times.

All I needed to do is show a single piece of paper. I wasn't sure if dropping off this paper was much more than that and I resisted exercising my inquisitive, proactive nature to dig to the bottom of this long line and the need for standing in it. After almost three decades in management consulting, I resisted, too, my natural inclination to suggest how the line could be made more efficient. I saw people go to the first window, the second, then the payment window a swimming pool away.

Window #2 is unattended for a spell.

An hour and a half passed. The petite woman ahead of me approached the first window. She chatted for a moment, then backed away and formed a new line at the second window.

I made out a woman in Window #1 behind Plexiglas. She motioned me forward.

I stepped by Loudmouth to the Plexiglas. I pulled out the critical piece of paper.

"I have an electrical inspection from DPNR, so you can come hook up my permanent meter."

Cool air leaked from under the window. The woman leaned in, pointing, "Next window."

"I go to the next window?"

Of course.

I moved behind Petite, who pulled out her phone. I overheard her say in Spanish that she wouldn't be making it back in time. She sighed softly and put her phone away.

While we two were waiting in this second line, Loudmouth went straight to the second window. That was it for me.

"Sorry, we're waiting here," I said.

"I ask you if you were gonna go."

I looked at Petite, who like everyone else remained poker-faced. I hadn't heard Loudmouth or the woman in Window #2 ask her to come forward.

"We were waiting to be called," I said.

"I ast whether anyone was goin go," she said louder.

How did I miss that? Is that even possible? I would have heard. If the woman in the second window had called, Petite would have moved forward.

I said to Petite, in Spanish, under my breath, seeking an ally, *she's been butting in line so much.*

She agreed quietly. Annoyance flashed through her eyes.

Loudmouth overheard me, and said loudly, "Oh, wow, she espeaka Spanish, like I won' understan'." She turned to her friend.

I cringed. How did I not catch that, her accent, that she was Puerto Rican, that she spoke Spanish? She went on and on for—what—ten, fifteen minutes about me, in Spanish, in English, in Spanglish, at large, talking about me in third person.

I buried myself in my book. She continued to rage on, taking her annoyance for WAPA and the line out on me. I was the scapegoat. I am white. But I was not operating out of privilege, I wasn't butting, she was. She looked around for corroboration. Everyone kept staring straight ahead.

The woman at Window #2 called Loudmouth, who was suddenly all charm as she approached the window, grabbed some forms, walked by me as if she's never seen me before.

Petite went to the window, and exchanged some papers. She moved away.

I was called. I shoved the electrical inspection and my ID under the Plexiglas.

"My electrical inspection from DPNR. I need to get a permanent meter installed and the temporary meter taken away."

The woman behind wrote something on the paper—initials, date.

"$30. Pay there." Her long bright red fingernail curled to her left, to Window #3.

"Can I pay here?"

"Other window."

"I have a credit on my account, can it be applied?"

"No. You need to go to the cashier." She sent an invoice through the mouse hole at the bottom, and kept my ID as security.

I went to Window #3. Petite was done paying just as I arrived. I slipped my bill under the window and a credit card.

"ID?"

"I'm sorry?"

"I need an ID." For the credit card.

"She's got it at the other window."

"I need it."

I walked back to Window #2 and leaned in. "She needs my driver's license to pay."

The woman slipped it under the window with my paperwork. "You're done."

"I'm done?"

I took my Driver's License and my electrical paper to the cashier.

Two hours in line for a two-minute transaction, a transaction that may mean that WAPA would visit me over the next two months and finish the job that had been two years in the making.

DANCE!

I LOVE to dance. No, I mean I LOVE to dance. Dancing is pure joy, with an underpinning of obsession, possibly compulsion egged on by an endorphin rush. After three hours and seven miles of steps, dripping wet, laughing my head off, I am in a state of mania.

As an older person, it's not easy to find places to dance. I used to count on weddings, but I stumble across those with less and less frequency. But on St. Croix, there is live music in a half dozen places almost every night. It's not all danceable, but I can find three or four events a week that are. This is one of the many reasons I love my time on St. Croix. I plan my weeks around when certain musicians play and stack those events with friends who will join me on the dance "floor," which may be grass or concrete or a deck. Every other Monday, I look forward to No Problemo with Steve Katz at Ziggy's— "the world's greatest gas station," with a bar and popup food events—where they share the stage with a half dozen other musicians, talented harmonica players, vocalists and bass players. I wear my Birkenstocks, but some dance barefoot.

Every Wednesday, I am at Cane Bay dancing to the Schindigglers, led by Kurt Schindler, arguably the most talented musician on the island. We dance in the grass, or sand-mud, under the red streetlights, fifty feet from the beach and an amazing sunset. My favorite is Sylvie's Place on Sunday once a month, where Kurt does his loop show. It's an interesting mix of people and the vibe is intense. Mama's Black Sheep comes down from Maryland for a few months every winter, and I seek them out several times during their stay. I will occasionally follow these groups to Bungalows or Cheeseburgers on other nights or at the St. Paddy's Parade or special occasions. Of course, winter months are packed with parades and festivals, and opportunities to kick up your flip flops.

I worked for the Peace Corps under Obama, as the inaugural Director of Innovation. Some 40% of the office was staffed by Returned Peace Corps Volunteers, who almost all shared a love of dance. As volunteers, they shake, shout, flail, and sway in villages all over the world, with joy and abandon, hang their arms and voices in the air. No one told them they had to, and it isn't on the application, but it seems an almost universal Peace Corps trait. And it works, since dance and music are ubiquitous. Every culture around the world has a beating drum and every volunteer will find it.

And I do too. I didn't serve in the Peace Corps, but spent a lot of time in other people's lives in other countries and cultures, and dance was an entrée, a way to engage and participate. I confess I dance because I can't help it. I will find my way onto the dance floor, wherever I am.

Aside from the joy and exercise of dance, dancing also demonstrates interest and willingness to be vulnerable. Like relishing food, dancing is a metaphor for life, an indicator of how a person takes on the world: as a game participant or passively on the sidelines.

I have always danced. First, alone, in my early teens, in the living room when no one else was home to Linda Ronstadt, Tijuana Brass, Hair, or Aquarius—the only "popular" music in my classical music home. In high school, I danced at dimly-lit mixers with whoever got over their shyness at the local boy school. Part of me was avoiding awkward chit-chat; I was never good at that. I was more comfortable on the dance floor than standing around and talking about . . . what? Our favorite subject?

    I danced a lot the summer of my junior year of high school when I went to Colima, Mexico, with American Field Service. I lived with a family of eight children, and there were *quinceañera* parties every other weekend at the Lion's Club. The only band in town played the same set of music every time. I took to the floor rather than stand around, or sit in one of the straight-back chairs which sternly lined the wall. The only drink served was Cuba Libres. I was too young to drink, didn't need a drink to dance, and never have. And I don't associate dancing with the disco rage of the seventies in New York City, and drugs, which I missed by a decade. I did see Saturday Night Fever and learned to hustle and danced for hours in college with sought-out partners whenever I could. After graduation, I took jazz dance taught by a skinny guy with a jerky neck and greasy curls, and Afro jazz from Tyrone, who seemed taller than he was, several times a week for a couple years. I learned a few moves and steps which I still count on. Despite all the time I spent in Brazil and throughout Latin America, my ear can't distinguish the rhythms of samba and salsa and merengue, and I can only fake Latin dancing when led by a patient and firm leader.

*   *   *

It is Latin Night at The Palms. Price, Carollyn and I are seated at a table for six. An ocean breeze enters stage left. Spotlights ricochet off the trunks of nearby palms. The blue pool is aglow, inviting, but empty. It's just backdrop.

    I'd been to this lazy Caribbean outdoor venue in the past. The food was mediocre, and I found it a tad sleepy. But I learned about Latin Night last week from my young in-the-know friend, Price. We dropped by after Mama's Black Sheep at Blues Backyard and caught the end of it. The vivacious band and dance instructors drew us onto the floor. Who could resist even in the wrong shoes? My heart pounded for more reasons than one.

    This week, we returned, and corralled others, all newish to the island, to introduce them to each other and to Latin Dance Night.

    Price, 20, is the granddaughter of a neighbor in the Hudson Valley. She contacted me last winter about moving to St. Croix. At first, I gave her loads of advice with enthusiasm, before reality set in, and I had misgivings. I told her grandmother I really didn't think Price should go; it would be too dangerous for a slight, young, inexperienced female traveler. But she persevered, arriving in May having secured a job and inexpensive, convenient rental. She made lots of friends, found additional work, has explored the far reaches of the island, is financially solvent and loves St. Croix. I was so wrong.

I met Sarah, 25, on Facebook. Sarah was recruited to work on the island. She bought a share of a plane I chartered to get her two dogs down to St. Croix with money—it turned out—she didn't have. Before we met, I spent a 40-hour work week helping her sort out travel portals, cars, accommodations. She knew so little about St Croix—and life in general— and was moving here. Since she arrived, Sarah frequently complains she never goes out with a deer-in-the-headlights look. Whether she doesn't know what to do or is scared or feels like she needs to spend every minute with her dogs, or doesn't have spare cash, I don't know. She seems miserable. Everything goes wrong. She's not asking for my help, directly, but her helplessness, her victim-hood, requires intervention. For better or worse, I decided to step in, to help her figure out how to love and embrace St. Croix. A few weeks ago, I included her for dinner and a play at the Community Theater. And tonight, Latin Night.

"I invited Sue, hope that's okay!" Sarah says, arriving a half hour late.

Sarah and Sue, her friend and neighbor, plunk down at the table and take out their phones. They spend the first fifteen minutes staring at their screens. I wonder what is so important that could have happened during the three-minute walk from Sarah's apartment. They have their backs to—don't even acknowledge—the excellent live band pouring their souls into mikes, strings, and skins. Sarah and Sue could have been anywhere. Home.

Sarah barely looks up when I introduce her to Price.

That was one of the main points: to introduce two young non-drinkers, which can be difficult on a duty-free island of retirees where rum runs from the faucet and drinks are served with a double pour in Styrofoam. I glance at Price in apology.

When the dance instructors come by with supplicating upturned palms, Sarah and Sue dismiss them saying, *No, no! I'm not going to dance* and go back to their phones.

Sarah orders the most expensive dish on the menu, even though she's broke. She could have bought a snorkel or groceries for a week for the price of the frozen Mahi she will eat.

She could be dancing for free.

The instructors won't sit out a single dance. They are eager even relentless to get us on the floor. They circle our table like turkey vultures and dance with each other if they can't scrape us off our seats. They are trying to drum up interest for their new studio in town.

I need zero encouragement. I am up and will be for the rest of the night.

Carollyn and Price are with me.

One, a-two, three, a-four.

But I am sad and frustrated by Sarah and Sue, who won't give it a go.

"I need another Corona," says Sue.

"I don't know how to dance," Sarah says.

That's why the instructors are here! And they are charming and enthusiastic and completely nonjudgmental, come in all heights and looks, depending on your penchant, although—to my astonishment— not one is Latino nor speaks Spanish. Garincha is the

Haitian with dancing eyes and broad smile; the short one is a Ukrainian Jew with an Israeli accent; and the tall guy who looks Russian is just a tall guy from Philadelphia. "They assume you don't know how to dance. They will count and step and twirl you to make you look like you are Dancing with the Stars."

But why not? I wonder what could hold them back. We are on a tiny island in the Caribbean, at Latin Night at The (very casual) Palms. The stakes are exceedingly low. No one else is here. It's a quiet night. Just us gals. No one cares whether you can dance.

Their apathy is a bit of a downer for the rest of us. I invited them tonight because Sarah said she knew no one and she never goes out. But here she is, instead of engaging, buried in this screen nonsense.

I clock three miles dancing and meet other interesting people— like a marine biologist who arrived six months ago and is acting and singing in the Community Theater. It turns out he did two tours of Peace Corps. True to form.

It's not just dance. It's about participating. In life. In general.

Yes, it is easy for me to say.

I am a bit of an extreme case. Participation is a compulsion. My upbringing emphasized engagement and curiosity; there was no loafing around, no tuning out. I was thrown into scads of situations that would intimidate the average bear. My parents introduce me to a room of strangers with something like, "Cynthia likes dogs too." I take it from there. I figure, if I'm going to spend an hour somewhere at some random party or on a bad date, I might as well learn something about underwater archaeology, astrophysics or restoring old books. I try to make the most of everything. I talk to everyone: the saleswoman at Home Depot, people standing in line at WAPA or behind the counter at Avis. At the farmer's market, I ask about a vegetable I don't recognize, whether I should toast green or yellow plantains, or how to make bush tea. I scour the bookstore for the shelf dedicated to local authors and books. I show up for parades, the agricultural fair and coconut festival, eat the local food, talk to makers.

Maybe I am describing a kind of *leaning in*. According to MacMillan online dictionary leaning in is to "accept challenges and seek responsibility." Close, but a little dour. Participating and being truly present, and really living in a place, can and should be joyful, full of adventure and laughter, especially when you make a mistake. It is taking responsibility for your own happiness, making things happen, and not being a victim.

When I ended up in St. Croix alone, I joined the Garden Club, Botanical Garden, Caribbean Museum of Art and Culture, Writer's Circle, Artists Guild, a book club, and a few years in when I had the time, started playing tennis again. I went to every benefit I could to meet the people who care about issues— spaying feral dogs, squashing domestic violence, coral reef restoration, getting fresh produce into local schools, recycling, leadership education. I go to Community Theater, pop-up master classes, art workshops and openings, readings, performances, and music of all kinds. And when it's appropriate and sometimes when it's not, I dance.

And I am usually the first one on the dance floor, alone. But not for long. I am one of those annoying people who try to get other people to dance, especially those who are tapping their feet or gyrating in their seat, who just need a little encouragement and whose partners are reticent. I want others to experience the joy too. Once moving, they realize how good it is for body and spirit.

If dancing is not your thing, then try bingo or charades or trivia, Scrabble, chess, hoops, if that's what's called for. Whatever. If you don't act, at least applaud those who do. Most people here find their niche and cause, volunteering for the World Ocean School, Ruff Start, or REAL Cruzan Cats, The Nature Conservancy, Women's Coalition of St. Croix, My Brother's Workshop, beach cleanups, St. Croix Environmental Association, St. Croix Turtle Project. They join the Yacht Club, start a recycling program, take pottery lessons or yoga at the museum. They play tennis or golf.

I met a man recently who has lived here for two years who decided that after he finishes renovating his house, he will sell it. St. Croix isn't for him. He didn't know who Fritz Henle was, had never been to the botanical garden or peeked into the King Christian Hotel or been out for local ice cream or even heard of the Coquito Festival. He's smart and educated, but perhaps he knows all he wants to. Unhappy Sarah will leave after a few months, too. It is by getting out of myself that I have learned to love St. Croix. I have learned, also, something about myself.

But I will leave Sarah and Sue to their (own) devices. Sarah doesn't want me to save her or solve her problems. This is how she will go through life, at least for the moment. I can't change that, and I guess it's not my job. People are different. I wish I could share my joy and make Sarah happy, but she doesn't seem to want to be.

But I can, and can't, help myself. The musicians are back. See you on the floor.

One, a-two, three, a-four.

ADULT PARADE

I approach from south of Frederiksted
early / not too early /
gauging parking / sun / start time—
a delicate calculation—
it starts sometime after 11—
not wanting to miss a moment /
a step / a shake
but not too early so as to lose enthusiasm
and vital signs in the heat
beneath the sun.
I seek shade-parking, easy escaping
required on account of
my housebound dog.

Things start happening
at the police station
across the sardined bus graveyard
and green gas station.
From there, in the neighborhoods
and along the road
vans / trucks / cars angle into the grass
clumps / gatherings of people
music blaring
headdresses and body-dresses:
oversized purple wings
glitter and gold
crimson and citrus yellow
parties in preparations.

I find friends.
We seek a spot
towards the end / the beginning
in shade / in sun near Ci Bo Ne.

We wait.

We wait.

We wait clasping our Corksicles
for the spectacular spectacle:
my first Adult Parade
the day following the Children's Parade,
the parade of parades.

With innocence / without urgency
the Adult Parade begins.
The Governor ambles by in breezy linens
a car honking.
A man approaches him
and for what seems a long time
locks him in a conversation. I think
he must have something important to say.
Then I hear him ask the Governor
in the middle of the parade
what form should I file?
What? Customer service on the run?
From the Governor?

I introduce myself to Bryan,
I am your neighbor in Princesse
We share a boundary.
He nods and shakes my hand.

And later statuesque Stacey Plaskett
dances by in USVI official madras
under an oversized hat.

Adorned trucks / flatbeds roll by
miniature houses
men / women dancing atop /
from openings / behind.

Drunk, spent shriveled white people
crawl the street
caulking up the flow
in love with their own revelry
a de / distraction
from the event beyond,
their inability to give others their time / due.

Throngs dance/parade/spin/shake/quiver
in non/traditional wear/feathers/costumes
performers worked for weeks/months/
since last year or paid a pretty penny.

Dancers/troupes/schools
businesses/institutions/causes/
in celebration.

We watch/witness/
peripheral to the exuberance
in awe of casual talent/
sheer joy/ecstasy
lack of in/exhibition
skimpy/scanty/feathery
throngs of thongs and
a winged yellow man
on the verge of taking flight.

WINDING DOWN

I am, like many on island, a snowbird, seasonal, and for a couple years, a COVID-bird. I arrive just after Thanksgiving and leave early April, give or take. Four months. As experts who study time note, time passes slowly and quickly all at once. And time in St. Croix is no exception. Time flies, but there are Groundhog Day weeks driven by schedules: musicians play in the same spot, same day, same time; Sandy Point is open only on weekends; some restaurants serve on certain days, or not. We count on these routines. There are punctuating moments, too, involving visitors, holidays, celebrations, or a jaunt to St John.

There is a moment about halfway through winter, mid-February, when I stop investing in home repairs, when I stop buying food for my (meager) pantry, knowing the joy of living with such purchases for the moment will not outweigh what eight months in briny breeze, unpredictable weather patterns, and Saharan dust will do. I look at the giant jar of Calamata olives and wonder what I was thinking.

And the capers?

A month before I leave, I ensure that I have seen everyone I want to see before it gets too late. I throw a dinner party to use up the olives and capers. A couple weeks out, my head is already home in the Hudson Valley, making and confirming plans for airport pickup, the first weekend home. I lock in time with Cliff to help me close the house in St Croix and secure a ride to the airport. This year, I am making my final list and trip to Home Depot to buy a battery charger for my new second-hand Mini Cooper, for an alternate solution for hurricane shutters, bags that absorb moisture in drawers so what I leave here will not be infested with permanent mold.

This morning, I drove my nephew Matthew to the airport. We had a great week of "firsts" and "lasts." His firsts, my lasts: the tidal pool walk and dip, Buck Island, Carambola beach, Cane Bay with Kurt Schindler on Wednesday (tall Matthew dancing with charming, petite German Ruta), snorkeling under the Frederiksted pier, honey lavender ice cream on the boardwalk, the long, hot, awe-inspiring hike out east, a lazy afternoon at Mermaid beach, night-time kayaking in Salt River Bay dragging nets through the water irritating and illuminating the bioluminescent organisms.

Matthew was helping me say goodbye to the island, doing things I hadn't done for a year or two, things I do mostly with visitors or when prompted. And although I had done most of these things before, I saw them through his eyes, and I experienced new things. A strong wind at Buck Island made the usual snorkel stop impossible, so we battled our way through the surf to a cove. After almost an hour of swimming against the current and into the wind, seeing nothing but stirred up sand, our guide turned us around. At that moment, an eagle ray rippled by, worth the trouble. On the way back, I spotted a gigantic sting ray scratching its belly on a round coral outcropping. The guide said it was the biggest he'd ever seen and said it was probably two hundred years old. (I looked up the lifespan of a sting ray later: 25 years. But no matter.)

    Now that Matthew is gone, I turn my attention to the essentials. I watch the water in my cisterns and discuss cleaning them with Cliff while I am away. I get out the chains and locks for the house and make sure I still have keys and codes. While I should be sleeping, I lie awake, and in my head, I move and tarp sofas, elevate furniture with woodblocks, bring pool and other outdoor furniture inside, bag pillows and comforters. I fold what I will bring home into a large suitcase, any clothes I care about. I use up the last milk and yogurt and think about whether I will leave the fridge on this time so I can leave the condiments behind, or whether I should find homes for them with friends. I make the last run to the dump with not just the usual garbage, but things I know I will not be using next year, that I no longer want in my life. I do laundry and fold and stow.

    Transitions. There's one at the beginning of the season, leaving my home in the Hudson Valley and arriving here. It's a week of closing and opening and fixing and arranging. And now, the reverse. They are tiresome and petty, and I wonder if they are necessary, the steps of mourning and renewal, cataloging and cleansing. There is anxiety and lists but there is also an appreciation and assessment. Of course, when you travel it is different. Those transitions are simpler, commemorated mostly by zipping a suitcase, airports, checking into a hotel.

    I had a similar transition at the front end, when moving from my life in the Hudson Valley to St. Croix, readying for four months of winter: putting up fencing and burlap to protect the evergreens so the deer don't make snacks of them; moving in outdoor furniture so it doesn't age more than it needs to nor blow across the field. We ate down leftovers from Thanksgiving and I roasted and froze heirloom pumpkins which were done with their decorating duties and would become fodder for Dexter in spring. Now, as I wind down in St. Croix, I start to think about how I left everything back home in the Hudson Valley, and what will need attention when I return.

    I'm fine leaving. People ask. I'm fine because the sargasm is piled high on Ha' Penny. Sandy Point is closing in a week. Iguanas lay broken on every road. It is just a couple degrees hotter, and oddly still or very windy, but these are not the gentle Christmas breezes. The lebbeck or women's tongue trees parched pods dangle, restless and rustling, spreading gossip in the wind. We no longer have the flash rains just before dawn to cool things down and green things up. The island is dry. Leaves are falling. The water-stressed hibiscus is covered in mites. The gardenia and another flowering plant I dug into the rock a couple months ago look like they will never get used to their new homes. I doubt, but hope, they will make it through the summer. Who knows what this summer will bring? I will be watching from a distance.

SKY, WATER, SAND

"Yes, we believe in the beach. We have always believed in the beach. Beaches are places of baptisms and funerals. Of bacchanal but also of solitude. But we did not consider the sea itself."

— Tiphanie Yanique, *Land of Love and Drowning*

BLUE AND BLUE AND BLUE

I am floating in a Rothko painting.

I find my calm
even when waves are ungentle
Saturdays
Sundays
under a hat
behind sunglasses
in the water
midday at Sandy Point.

Rothko stopped naming (and framing)
only numbered and colored
allowing the viewer
maximum interpretation.
I search but it's not
Blue Divided by Blue
not
Blue Divided by Grey
No 14 White and Greens in Blue
718B
Blue and Marine
Hand Painted Blue on Blue
nor Moodboardmix XI.

I am floating in a painting Rothko never made.

Close, maybe inverted
too/still. I am in fields of blue
hard to name
hard to frame:

Impossibly intimate/
infinite.

But I will try:

I will frame this view/
these waters
over and over
but never capture
what it is to be in it/them.
One has to be:

here

in this/nature's canvas
Modernist/Abstract/Expressionist
seduced by/reduced to essentials:
sky
water
sand.

In the distance: a brown-gray missile
tuck-drops/plunge-dives/
emerges with a gallon of water
and a fish
in its expandable chin/beak sack.

Give me an excuse just to be.

I am in
a Rothko un-painting
of saturated shimmering blues
wave-lifted/lowered.

When I am not floating
but on the beach
I will wait until the walkers and
disappointed snorkelers
are out of view,
will aim left of the beer-drinking
noodle-hugging group
to try to capture *this*.

Maybe choose to include the
two kayaks, a distant sailboat
the bright orange floaty tube,

as they visually punctuate the seascape.

I will wait for them to walk by/leave/
get out of the water
before I take a meditative/undulating video
I may post/send/watch later.

Someone/Pantone already named
these blues.
I say: unfair play.
No, Pantone, you cannot claim/call this/
it is not
Swedish or Mediterranean or Curaçao blue.
St. Croix's coastal waters own these
colors/bands/sweeps.
They are not Cool Blue/Mint
but passion-filled serenity.

I am in awe
of what is left after
red, orange, yellow light is absorbed as
Deep Peacock, Cornflower hues
are reflected and
captured in hundreds of viewfinders
and in the retinas of other bouncing surf souls.
This unnatural blue hue of the waters
differs from/clashes with the powdered sky
found on a different Pantone color card.
With sun and clouds and waves changes/
is never still/mesmerizes.

In its clarity it is not Blue Mist
nor Bonnie's.
Nor does it belong to Robin.
This blue is not of a Lake, no,
but, yes, squeals Teal.

In the shallows, the sand adds its piece/peace.
There is yellow, too: so, Turquoise.
How does Tiffany own this tone
which defies boxing/framing?

Rothko, a self-proclaimed myth-maker and
self-lifetaker declared:
the exhilarated tragic experience
is for me the only source of art
but I submit: these waters
inspire/d.
Or they are so magnificent
re/creating is unnecessary/impossible.

Rothko viewed myth as a replenishing resource
for an era of spiritual void.
Where/what is myth in these blues
replenishing with unbound generosity
all souls
without apology
making us stupid in the riches for alone
bearing witness?

What myth are we making?
Who will paint this?
Whose picture/view do I occupy?

No temperance for me.
I will not abstain.
I am all in:
I am drunk
by these waters
buoyed/a buoy
without a tether/mooring
un/secured only by my wonder
watching/allowing my toes—
one with a shiner from the morning walk
on a different, rocky beach—
to mar the view from
four feet away.

What more could one want/need?

And yet today there is more.
An extra dividend in the form of a visitor,
a seabird swaddled in

myths of the Rothko variety:
Christian and heraldic iconography
now a few breast strokes away.
Pelicanus occidentalis,
a 30-million-year-old
prehistoric Old World question mark.
Its leathery feathery form interrupts
the horizon line.

We are very New World/Modernist here
despite this ancient visage watching me:
tucked snug smug with a beak a mile—
no, really, a foot—long.
(That is long enough.
No reason to embellish.)

Its beak tip skims at 90 degrees
the water's surface
while it watches me
as I it.
I approach.
It stays its ground/water
atop the darkest blue band
not 15 feet away.

This lone pelican defies its species,
or not.

Perhaps it has chosen to be gregarious
with me,
will hunt cooperatively
perhaps expects this human to scare up silver
translucent flitting fish
which occasionally jump above the surface
to look-see.

I swim towards the folded bird.

It stays
coy/unfazed until
in a fractured moment
I have crossed a/the line/am too close.
It spreads its seven-foot span.
I feel wings' breath.
I am for a moment in its flee(t)ing shadow.
Pelicanus lands and finds
a new social circle beyond
in shallower/less threatening waters.

I am alone again
floating in a Rothko un-painting:
Number Infinity

Blue and blue and blue.

PELICAN COVE

My neighbor Aziyza recommended a nearby beach and made it sound simple: a two-mile drive down the hill past Five Corners. I found it on Google maps but couldn't figure out how to access the beach, a problem tourists have, but I shouldn't two months in to living on St. Croix.

I tried to get to the beach via The Nature Conservancy's headquarters in Little Princess, through the open gate, beyond the NO TRESPASSING signs. The two-story plantation house had not fared well in the last hurricane, but a functioning-looking truck indicated activity. I didn't see the beach or a trail, and left before I caused trouble. I doubled-backed through the nearby neighborhood heading down a sandy road with no demarcations between a couple houses to a dead end. A gang of barking canines kept me honest, and in the truck. I could see sky—the ocean—beyond a row of bushes on the other side of a yellow house with red shutters.

A woman emerged, peering at me through small glasses. I was likely trespassing. "Hi! Sorry to bother you. Is there access to the beach through here?"

Without a shred of charm and minimal movement, the woman pointed at the dense sea grape tree forest behind her. "There was a path there, but I think it's grown over. You can just go here," she said, pointing at her yard.

"Thank you! Thanks so much! Okay if I park here?" I couldn't tell where the street and her property began and ended. She shrugged. I looked out the window at the crowding canines. "Are they friendly?"

"I don't know," she said, seeing them as if for the first time. "They belong to the neighbors." She turned away. I gathered the water bottle I refill and refrigerate each day, a plastic bag, my phone. I gave the dogs time to scatter before I leashed and let Dexter out of the backseat. We raced to the beach before they returned.

The ocean was right there beyond the bushes. I took a good look around to remember where I'd parked, recording the woman's house, noting the colorful chairs and bushes by the water. She had a simple but enviable setup thirty feet from the surf, her house elevated a few feet. I wondered how her home withstood the winds and how long she'd been there, hidden away, at the end of the road. I wondered if she ever left.

Dexter and I headed east on the narrow beach, towards Christiansted, which basked in the late afternoon light in the distance. Lush, exuberant, succulent bushes packed an impenetrable green wall to our right. We walked maybe a half mile, alongside what I assumed to be The Nature Conservancy property. I could not see the building from the beach, but guessed it was buried a few hundred feet in. Dexter and I continued beyond to a utility clearing fifty feet wide which cut straight through the brush perpendicular to the ocean with deliberation and recency. It stirred in me an irrational fear of contamination, electrocution or landmines, a line I wouldn't cross. That clearing became our turnaround point.

It was a lovely, private, humanity-less walk, if a bit shorter than I'd hoped, and not much of a swimming beach, which I accepted, since Dexter doesn't really allow me to swim on our walks anyway. As we arrived back to the yellow house, we stole across the yard to the pickup, not wanting to bother the woman—or dogs—again.

The next time I tried to get to Pelican Cove, I sought access on the other, western end indicated on the map. When I found it, I was surprised this vegetative tunnel had made the map. It didn't seem an official entrance. An unofficial dump in a clearing to the right appeared alive, fresh, growing, as if someone had just been there, or was still there, maybe slept there on the abandoned mattress. Broken glass, dog poop and mud puddles kept me careful about where I placed my flip-flopped feet, but my eyes darted into the bushes for activity, a feral dog, a person. A presence was palpable—and threatening. I moved quickly and softly, feeling that I, too, probably didn't belong. I didn't want to feel scared, but I couldn't control my racing heart.

When I head to the beach, I try to remember not to bring anything with me, curse then hide whatever I have, not sure if the valuable and I are safer with it on my person or in the truck. I lock the truck and hold the key in my hand in case someone or a dog comes out of nowhere, ready to make a run for it. Do men have these same fears? I doubt it. Most women I speak to do. Many wouldn't go alone to a beach on St. Croix.

An abandoned two-story hotel, windows and doors blown out by a hurricane—unclear which, and how long ago—and a couple trailers off to the left, held the vistas hostage. When I returned, occasionally another dog walker was there, or someone milling around the ruins. I met one of the trailers' inhabitants one afternoon after a downpour. He emerged with a beer and a folding chair to watch a double rainbow over the ocean as if it were a ballgame. That day, I'd left my dead phone in the car.

I'm not sure why I continued to go there, other than out of necessity and ignorance. I had already learned that walking in neighborhoods or on shoulder-less roads presented other issues—generally in the form of snarling dogs and cars that either whipped by too fast or slowed down. Ultimately, that beach entrance wasn't worth the risk or anxiety. Rather than providing a relaxing respite at the end of the day, the adrenaline rush put me on edge.

I eventually found alternative access, at the parking lot at The Palms resort. *Duh.* By law in St. Croix, even private developments and gated communities must provide public access to the beach. Between Calabash Real Estate and The Palms HOTEL GUESTS ONLY pool with bright blue cushions, welcoming, plush white sand carpeted a grove of coconut palms and the way to the beach. What a relief. This was what Aziyza must have

meant.

Pelican Cove became a regular end-of-day beach walk, a weekly routine, close and long enough to provide good exercise for both Dexter and me, when time didn't allow us to go elsewhere, like on weekends, when we headed to the East End for an early morning hike.

Under the coconut trees, I kick off and leave my flip-flops, a revisited calculation each time since the beach beyond the sandy entrance requires vigilance, rough with shells and rocks and the broken root stubs of toppled palms, and the occasional piece of glass not yet tumbled and worn. I don't mind being forced to look down, to take in the array of treasures the reef has surrendered, but I like to look out, too, over the mottled, colorful shallow waters without having to worry. In some parts, where it's possible, I walk in the surf, to at least touch and savor the sea, feel its pulse around my ankles. Dexter plunges, seeking relief from the heat. He tests, again, to see if the water is still salty until I reel him back and pour chilled fresh water from the bottle into my cupped hand. He laps it up until he gags, then coughs. We go on for a bit and do it again.

We walk beyond Pelican Cove Condos, where the vegetation was cleared to install rows of two-story buildings angled to the coast, each with their own patio-deck. Despite proximity to the ocean and magnificent views, I rarely see anyone on their deck.

I vow to never take beauty for granted.

We are on the northeast side of the island, and so mostly in the shade at that hour. The blues and rust-colored seaweed are deep and vivid. Swerving and downed coconut palms lean and bend over the ocean and against the sky like contortionists. Soft green mossy seaweed carpets square concrete pylons with angling rebar, possible remnants of an industrial dock.

One afternoon, as Dexter and I approached the beach that belongs to the yellow house with red shutters, a fit, youngish man in blue trunks plunked himself down on the sand. Just as he did so, a slight wind picked up and blew off his baseball cap. He leaned back to grab it, but it bounced away just out of reach. He leaned further and further trying not to touch the sand, or get up, but it kept dancing away, until he fell flat on his back.

"Fuck!" he exclaimed with an unvarnished violence. He got up, brushed off, and saw me. "Oh, sorry, 'scuse the—"

"No worries," I said. Just at that moment, three dogs emerged from the bushes behind him. "Are the dogs—?" I was about to ask if they were *friendly* but before I could, a mid-sized white husky mix raced forward and lunged at Dexter's throat snarling wildly. I screamed instinctively and yanked Dexter back which stalled the dog for the moment we needed to retreat. I scooped up a couple stones, running backwards, and forwards looking back, in the direction from which we'd come, dragging Dexter who was all resistance. The husky and its sidekick were barking and coming after us.

"Go home!" I commanded, lowering my voice an octave and with as much confidence as I could muster. "Go home!" They didn't go home, but did stop in their tracks, alert. Were they the same dogs Dexter and I had encountered at the dead end on the other side of the yellow house weeks earlier? Was he the neighbor? Our afternoon walk was curtailed. But more, this beach I had worked so hard to find now had a red flag. I would have to watch for those dogs every time we passed through.

Beyond that spot is a stretch of greenery, and a narrow beach, one that doesn't encourage swimming, such that one comes to expect no humans. From the beach, at least, no buildings or pathways are visible. But, over the course of a few weeks, a woman sitting in a folding beach chair appeared, nestled up against the bush smoking a cigarette. She was usually on the phone, never said hello, did not even look our way, although we were only a dozen feet away. Perhaps she felt as proprietary as I had become, but on an island where people are friendly, and at such proximity, her lack of acknowledgment felt odd.

A few weeks went by when I saw only the empty chair, pushed up against the vegetation. One day the chair was gone.

Then, in late February, in that same stretch, around the curve, we came across a broad, dark-skinned, dark-haired muscular man with long swim trunks gripping a spear, a net, and a bucket to go fishing on the shallow reef. I wasn't sure if fishing was permitted, given how delicate and endangered the reefs are. I greeted him in Spanish, which always surprises Latinos since I don't look the part. We chatted for a bit. He was Dominican, and his family was camping further down.

Then, his eyes narrowed, in English, in a different tone, he said, "You sexy." His spear and proximity took on a different aspect.

I had spent a lot of time in Latin America as a young, tall blonde, long before many places became overrun with tourists who looked like me. I learned to put on a stone face, to not let anyone in, but here, now, I had already let my guard down. When he said that, I turned away, ending the conversation, erecting a wall on the beach. I told him, in Spanish, I was his mother's age and strode away, with determination in my step, without letting on that I felt threatened. Why can't I, at my age, enjoy a walk on a beach, a little conversation, without a man making me feel unsafe?

At the end of our walk, adjacent to the utility line, Dexter and I came upon a small encampment with a half dozen people—the fisherman's family, sitting under a blue plastic tarmac, a transient shelter they'd carved out of the bush. I exchanged greetings with a leggy, slouched woman sitting on a plastic white chair at the front.

"I told *mi esposo* that he would meet a mermaid," she said, with a wide, gap-toothed grin," and he should go home with her!" She laughed and slapped the air.

I smiled and pretended I didn't understand her.

Heading back, thankfully, the fisherman was hundreds of feet offshore getting dinner.

    I didn't return to the beach for a week, hoping the family—and spear-guy—would be gone and that they took all their garbage with them.

    When my friend Karen visited St. Croix, in early March, I paused work on the house and treated her to a different beach every day, sometimes two. On her penultimate day, I took her to Pelican Cove. She'd been on St. Croix almost a week and, I think, figured it would be just another beach—some combination of sand and water and sky, so left her phone in the car. When we came through the coconut grove near the hotel—which, it turns out, Jim Weber and Harry Ehle planted in the middle of last century—she was blown away, that even number six on my list, my convenient down-the-road, almost-in-town beach was breathtaking and unexpected in its own way, with a distinct personality and profile all its own. I suggested she sit on the beach while I walked Dexter, but she was game for a little more exercise.

    Karen had gotten used to my trepidations about other dogs and Dexter, although I sensed she thought I was overly cautious. As a New Yorker, dogs she knew were socialized to be friendly. In St Croix, many are rescues and unpredictable, and some are encouraged to be aggressive guard dogs, even trained to bite. I could not take any chances.

I threw my gaze ahead, looking out for the dogs. The indirect sun beyond the palms, the condos, softened the late afternoon. The waves curled. The tide was lower than I'd ever seen; sea urchins with long black spikes lay wait in tidal pools like UFOs. Others, spineless, white and hollow, lay on the sand nearby.

Dexter tugged me forward and then stopped and sniffed something. I caught up to him, while keeping his head away from a swarm of flies descending on an ambiguous pile of entrails, light gray skin glistening and smooth, what I recognized as part of a porpoise maybe, but I will never know for sure. I pulled Dexter away and we continued, but my curiosity to this day keeps revisiting what it could have been.

We arrived where the Dominican family had camped, leaving plastic chairs and the tarmac, a cage of some sort, chip bags, water bottles. I was saddened by their casual degradation of the pristine spot they had enjoyed.

We turned back, and where I'd encountered the fisherman and ambiguous entrails, against the tree line in the shade, a thin man, fully-clothed, with wild white eyes against his dark, gaunt face and prominent cheekbones, sat in a ball with his arms gripping his knees near his head. Where had he come from? I saw no visible path. He wasn't at the beach for a swim, but huddled, pulled inward, away from something, everything.

From the water's edge, twenty feet away, as far as we could be, I called, "Good afternoon."

He was shouting, mumbling, all at once, fast, without looking our way. "Don't talk to me, don't talk to me. You don't see me . . ." with an intensity, an edge that sent shivers down my spine. I would always see him, of course, never forget him. Karen's face shut down. An experienced traveler, she too knew we needed to keep moving. He was disturbed and disturbing.

"Let's go," I said under my breath. We had never stopped but picked up our pace. A few steps later, I glanced over my shoulder to make sure he wasn't following. I was scared but also embarrassed for St. Croix. The day, the week, was spoiled by this encounter. I had tried to put St. Croix's best foot forward for Karen. I had curated everything for her, had driven down the prettiest roads, made her look a different direction if I knew a sofa had been dropped off on the side of the road. This was not the note I'd hoped to end on.

When we got back to the truck, a uniformed man walked by the hood of the pickup, through the parking lot. I jumped out.

"Excuse me. Are you security?"

"Yes."

"I just wanted to let you know there's a guy on the beach beyond the condos."

"I been looking for him. We seen him before." I described where he was, but thought it was further than this guard's jurisdiction. He was at least a half mile from the condos. Nonethe-

less, the guard's presence and concern were reassuring.

With three uncomfortable encounters in as many weeks, I vowed I wouldn't return to Pelican Cove for a spell. I didn't want to have my healing walks to take on a tenor of fear and suspicion, even if nothing actually transpired. I did not want to be controlled by aggressive men or dogs or random insanity.

A couple days later, after Karen left, against my better judgment, I returned to Pelican Cove with Dexter in the morning, reasoning that I couldn't possibly run into a problem in the morning. And I didn't have time to go elsewhere nor later in the day.

Beyond the condos, and before the yellow house with red shutters, a long and low-slung house sat a hundred feet from the water, with NO TRESPASSING and PRIVATE signs. The house's color was a hue that came from another era, another world, harsh, clean, bright, septic, light green that might have been used on bathroom tile in the seventies. Or my Crocs.

The house seemed to be comprised of different living chambers connected by a long, six-foot-high wall with small rectangular rhythmic perforations, recalling the pigeonholes of Turkey's Cappadocia cave formations, but were really just block. On one end, the windows were covered with vertical metal security bars, and on the other, the windows were shuttered with metal hurricane panels on tracks. The house appeared boarded up, ready for a hurricane, possibly unoccupied, curiously, during high season. There was something understated, almost elegant, and yet menacing about this house, which cut a profile at sunset, surrounded by tall, sloping coconut palms, some headless, and a slender angling Norfolk pine which seemed to hang from the sky rather than emanate from the earth. Despite the house's unnatural color, it was inexplicably comfortable, natural, in its surroundings.

Near the ocean, Dexter made a habit of sniffing his way up the short set of irrelevant stairs into the enthusiastic shrubbery which render the steps impassable. The surf-softened stone wall appeared to be sea-bound and suggested there might have been a longer wall at one time. The abbreviated wall sounded an alarm for the house, and maybe many houses built close to the sea, close to sea level.

Dark, powdery termite lines wandered up and across the wall of a small cottage, of the same green color, offering an abstract canvas, and an omen.

As we approached the sea-foam green house, that day, I saw life: a skinny, overly-tan, white man stood beside a West Indian, with a round face and glasses, leaning on a rake, in the yard, in conversation. The sand below the palms had fresh rake lines.

"Good morning! Is this your house?" I asked.

The two men stared at me.

"Is this your house?" I asked again. The white guy glowered; the man with the rake pointed at the white man, as if to say, *it's his house*.

"Do you live here?" I asked. I was being too forward, but I had walked by this house on this beach so many times and never seen anyone, although at that moment I vaguely remembered weeks before someone perched on the stone wall with a cigar who could have been this man.

"I just wanted to warn you that there was a strange man down the beach a few days ago."

The white man approached, and stood in my orbit, a little too close. "What'd he look like? Black or white?"

"Black." Suddenly, I felt uncomfortable, and regretted that I played into his hand. There were different kinds of people on this island, waves of settlers, with different educations and sensibilities, and prejudices. I wasn't sure—actually, I was—where this was going.

"Probably drugged up. Didn't used to be that way. People stayed out of the way of one another. Things have gotten worse, so violent."

"Well, I've been here many times and never had a problem."

"I had some crazies on my roof last night," he said.

"On your roof?"

"Yeah! I woke up in the middle of the night and these people were on the roof! I took out the hose to spray them, to make the roof slippery so they would slip and hurt themselves." He laughed.

"What? Did you ask them to get down?"

"They wouldn't get down!"

"That is crazy." Up close, his tan was a bleeding collage of freckles and brown spots. He was angular, maybe even anorexic, unhealthy, one of those people who, if you unzipped them would be green inside, maybe the color of his house.

We talked about dogs—I think he liked my sporting setter—and his five-acre fenced-in lawn on the other side that he mowed himself.

"Adrian. Adrian Platt," he held out his hand.

It was early March 2020; COVID was just breaking in the U.S. There weren't any cases on St. Croix yet, but I wasn't sure if I should shake this guy's hand, but I was afraid not to. Was he testing me? Personal space was already political.

"Cynthia," I said, taking his bony hand. "Are you related to Lee Platt?" I asked. Lee was the owner of the 1 Pearl property I almost bought. Adrian embodied how I'd imagined Lee Platt to look.

He shook his head slowly, studying me. "No. No relation."

Adrian stepped back to his perch on the sandy crest. "My mother's last name was Mead," he added, for reasons I didn't yet understand. As bad as I am with names, I remembered Adrian Platt and Mead long enough to search online when I got home.

"Why are you so optimistic?" he asked.

What an odd question. I consider myself social and curious, but optimistic? I was just being friendly, without condoning his racism and politics.

He stepped forward, even closer than before, and his close, deep-set beady eyes pierced mine. "I wanna tell you something," he said. He looked around as if he were sharing a secret. "That Biden is a crook. He's—" he leaned in and spit-whispered, "*dangerous.*"

I laughed and backed out of his misty sea breath. "Well, I'm not going to get into that discussion." I moved away. "I've overstayed. Nice to meet you."

Dexter and I continued a few hundred feet when I sensed a presence behind me. I turned. The gardener had followed in his awkward, too-big rubber boots. He seemed non-threatening; he was seeking me out, not stalking me. I pulled Dexter in and allowed him to catch up.

"I just want to tell you dat guy, Adrian, he crazy. He made all dat up, about the people on de roof." His index finger circled near his temple. I was glad for the visuals, because his accent was thick.

"He seemed a little off. Are you okay? He seemed scary to me. Racist. I hope he treats you alright."

"Yeah. He pay me even when they no work. I take him grocery shopping. He rich. He got extra rooms he could rent and make a lot of money, but he don't."

"Well, I don't know. . . You take care, okay?"

Dexter and I kept walking. On our way back, they were gone.

Later I looked up Mead Platt and found a Helen, of Hartley Farms in Harding, New Jersey. According to the *Morristown Daily Record*, September 25, 2017:

> An accomplished equestrian, side-saddle fox-hunter, artist and champion of farmland and open-space preservation, Helen Mead Platt was born in Madison in 1922. Close family members included philanthropist Marcellus Hartley Dodge, husband of Geraldine Rockefeller Dodge, whose foundation donates millions to Morris County and New Jersey arts and education

programs annually.

Platt's family first came to Morris County in the 1840s. She was the great-granddaughter of Marcellus Hartley, who founded what later became the Remington Arms Company.

There were guns in the family, for sure, and also hunting dogs—like Dexter. Most uncanny is that my father ran the Geraldine R. Dodge Foundation for 25 years. When I called him, my father said that Adrian's mother and her husband were considered one of the wealthiest couples in the country in their time. Noted in the obituary, she had seven children, including a son named Adrian. Here he was tucked away on St. Croix, whispering nonsense to passersby, hosing down nonexistent people on his roof and not renting perfectly good rooms to strangers.

HA' PENNY

My regular walking beach became Ha' Penny, also known as Machineel Bay. It is a solid, no-nonsense beach on the south shore a twelve-minute drive, offering an unencumbered mile walk each way under a big sky. The long stretch of sand without shade is visible from beginning to end, so has fewer surprises than, say, Pelican Cove or Chenay Bay.

Notably, I drive by 1 Pearl every day to get there, and peer down the driveway. Sometimes the gate is open, and I think about whether I should drive down and see who bought it and what happened to that seductive structure. But I drive on.

We enter off south shore road, turning in at the pink pillars onto a dirt road. After navigating the potholes, driving by Dan the Music Man's goat farm, trying to look past the sofa and mattress and tire recently dumped in the middle of the road, I pull into the parking area by the water and note who else is there. There are a dozen regulars, people I come to expect on certain days at certain hours. About half show up with dogs of their own. I've learned which dogs and owners are friendly, which to avoid, and try to time my visits accordingly. I breathe a sigh of relief if no one is there. We like the beach to ourselves.

My favorite parking place is in the bushes. But if others are there, I park looking out over the water. If there's not a fisherman, there is a leggy snowy egret (not to be confused with the smaller cattle egret who follows lawnmowers, in groups, snapping up insects) standing in the gentle surf, picking its way through the shallows. I wonder if it is a territorial male, with claim to that spot, or whether several take turns in a civilized agreement. This tall creature with a snake-like neck stretches this way and that surveying the waterscape in slow motion before it commits to move its feet. Emerging from the car, Dexter will immediately "point," tail out, tense, pull in its direction. I'll point my phone at it to snap a photo but will encourage Dexter to come along to the beach beyond without disturbing the emblem of grace, although if we've startled it or gotten too close, the moment it takes to flight has its own poetry.

A couple hundred feet in is a large, naked sea-sculpted log with soft majestic curves rolling and repositioning with the tide. It's always on the move. I keep meaning to send a photo of this one, crafted by nature, the sea, to my friend Eames, who has an annual global bench competition.

Dexter, an English Setter, a bird dog, who knew only the Hudson Valley's fields and woods, adapts his love of rabbits to chasing and extracting crabs, digging wildly, butt in the air, tail wagging, kicking up sand like a cartoon character in a comic strip. He races out ahead then stops every thirty feet to stick his nose down a ghost crab hole—to my amusement and a smidge of annoyance—and if it smells active to him, digs furiously, kicking sand fifteen feet out. He digs, stops to sniff again to reassess the situation, and digs some more, unless I yank, taking advantage of a pause. Sometimes, I will see the translucent, yellowish, be-spectacled creature escape from a backdoor, running to the ocean, sideways, at high speed, and float away before Dexter comes back up for air. If I allow him to dig a second or third round, it is generally over for the crab. Dexter, now a foot underground, butt high in the air, may jerk up with the crab in his mouth, as surprised as I, having been pinched by the little guy who has a lot more at stake. I am glad to have Dexter on a leash, so I can pull him away before he catches the crouching, quaking crustacean, to spare a life, but also so we can keep moving and I get a modicum of exercise. If Dexter had it his way, we wouldn't go anywhere. This year, it seems, the crabs have become a little casual, or lazy, in their burrows, or Dexter has become more skilled. Or maybe I'm too slow to intervene. He snagged more in a week than all of last year.

I keep my eyes open for teal fishing nets and ropes to carry home for an art project I have in the works, which also might spare a turtle from getting caught and mangled. Some nets are too buried and laden with fan corals to extract. When I get home I put them in a bucket with bleach before I hang them on the wall.

A small flock of semipalmated sandpipers, Wilson plovers, or royal or least terns may be making their way down the beach, too, spaced evenly in the dunes or dancing along the shoreline. There are dozens of shorebird species on the island; who knew there were so many varieties and how hard they are to identify? (And thank you, Toni Lance for identifying these.) Dexter may decide to stalk them, eager to scare them up and chase them over the water. I brace myself so we both don't get whiplash from the leash. They fly over the water briefly and return to shore, a few yards behind or ahead.

There may be a small boat a ways out, silhouetted by the morning sun, lulling in the tide, or a speed boat skipping over the water towards shore. A large oil tanker, coming from the refinery beyond and out of view, may emerge, separating from the rocky outcropping at the far end of the beach and will pull along the horizon slowly.

At that same bluff, a brown pelican, or a pair, will coast on six-foot wings, high overhead, or just above the water for a few hundred feet. The brown pelican, a regular sighting on Ha' Penny, was on the endangered species list from 1970 to 2009, having suffered the effects of pesticides. After DDT was banned, pelicans made a stunning comeback and are now in the category of "least concern." I, nonetheless, find every spotting precious and reach for my phone, hoping for a shot of one dropping for fish in the tide, or a view of them flying in tandem tantalizingly close to the water's surface.

A couple times a year, we witness a large stallion and equestrian racing down the beach, and a distant, trailing assistant with a water bucket. I pull Dexter into the dunes away from the charging cavalry, to make sure we don't startle the horse, or get trampled, and to get a good view of the passing drama. Once, when I was getting water delivered for my pool, I recognized the young man as a horseback rider from months earlier on

the beach. Beautiful horses are left on grassy patches and medians along roadsides in unexpected places all over the island. A common and welcome sight, we hear about and see the beautiful animals getting hit by cars or being neglected. Four or five are out on the large lawn by the public swimming pool adjacent to Sion Distillery, in the Plaza East area, with water buckets usually turned on their sides on a sweltering day. We pass them every day.

    A couple years ago, Dexter and I were walking on the beach and he spotted movement. It turned out to be a baby turtle, and the first of dozens making their way from a nest under a tree near the (only) hotel. A whole unruly army of baby turtles was making their way towards the water, so small that my own footprints compromised their progress. They flapped around wildly like moths at a light, until they hit the surf and were carried away. I was thankful to have Dexter on a leash, as always, or he would have "played" with them like he does with the crabs and the coconuts.

    We comb that beach almost every day, note its changes. Dexter found the same dead fish for a month every time, even though the entire coastline had altered. The beach itself is alive, moving, shaping, growing, shrinking. From one day to the next, and as the seasons and years pass, I am amazed how much it morphs. Last year, much of it was washed away

during a big storm. Dexter and I wallowed in the surf through the pervasive sargassum piled on what was left of the beach below a four-foot sand cliff; hundreds of ping pong ball eggs were visible in the crevices and in the water. Did they die then, or were they already dead, fried during the hot summer?

    This year, the beach is long and wide all over again, with no evidence of that time, although the colorful lean-to made of collected garbage and palm fronds was mostly obliterated.

    One morning, I set off with Dexter, happy to be alone. I wouldn't have to negotiate with any unleashed dogs or intolerant owners. Just as we headed out, a Wrangler pulled in next to our car. A couple got out. They began to walk about a quarter mile behind us.

    I kept up the pace for the exercise but also so the couple wasn't on top of us. But we lost ground with all that crab hunting and when I stopped to give Dexter drinking water, so they were closing in. Then, as we reached the far end of the beach, silhouetted by the angling sun, I saw a lone man on the beach. I could barely make him out. But he took me by surprise, since there had been no other vehicles in the parking lot. He was walking into the surf, the spray caught by the sun, the sun ricocheting off his muscular chest. He fell forward into the water to swim. Really, no cause for concern, it just threw me, since I hadn't noticed him until the last second. I turned around.

Within a few hundred feet, I bumped into the couple.

"I was going to tell you to be careful," the guy, who seemed in his mid-thirties, said. "This beach is dangerous. Puerto Ricans come in through the bush." We fell into step together. He started to enumerate the crimes and risks. He'd grown up on St. Croix, moved away, returned, had a bunch of businesses.

I didn't want to let on that I'd been nervous, but he gave me reason to be. And I didn't want to believe I should be scared because there were *Puerto Ricans*. I wondered if he was just another alarmist or if there really was cause for concern, how much was just the long memory of all that has occurred over decades. On a small island, you know people who get mugged and assaulted. You recognize the places. It's not distant and anonymous.

When I told Jill, who'd lived on the island for half a century, about some of my experiences, she said, "You shouldn't walk the beaches alone." All these beautiful, empty beaches are empty because . . . everyone's scared? "A woman and two children were burned in their car on Ha' Penny."

"When?"

"Not too long ago." I later Googled it: Ten years ago.

It's a matter of time, of probabilities, I suppose. I am over sixty, have traveled, often alone, all over the world, and now I have to worry about being assaulted here on my home-island? That's crazy making. The beaches, the lifestyle, make this island special.

"I can't live my life in fear," I asserted.

"I'm just saying you need to be cautious," she implored, "smart."

"You're telling me I can't walk a beach alone, ever? None of the beaches?"

"I wouldn't," she says. And she doesn't. In fact, I have never seen her on a beach. "And you should put a gate at the bottom of your driveway. You should plant bougainvillea and century plant at the backdoor. Plants that cut." Jill has an elegant voice, even and precise, not quite an accent, but one that has credibility and naturally commands. And she knows the house and the neighborhood. That phrase, *plants that cut,* stuck with me.

A park ranger said that drugs are dropped off on the beach at night. I've never seen anything that could be construed as a drug deal, but I started walking Ha' Penny more in the morning than at sunset.

When I asked carpenter Daniel, partner of the Toast waitress, and who lived across the street, what he thought about Ha' Penny, he said, "We go there all the time with our pit bulls."

"When do you go?"

"Late afternoon." Duly noted.

"Is it safe?"

"Sure," he said, while adjusting a kitchen cabinet. "You take your machete with you, don't you?" he added, without a shred of irony or a smile.

I started to carry an air horn, to prevent or break up a dog fight, to startle.

I wanted the facts. I searched *homicides St. Croix*. In 2019, there were 22 homicides listed chronologically, mixed in with those on St. Thomas, as per Virgin Island Police Department notes in an indifferent, bare-bones way. Only one seemed to not be gang-related, revenge or personal: a situation in which two women were stopped in their car going east. One was raped and killed; the other escaped. The guy was caught. Even one a year is unacceptable, on this tiny, mostly friendly island, but somehow it set my mind at ease. In 2024, 13 homicides occurred on St. Croix. I could not find listings for stabbings, robberies, thefts, assaults on beaches, only murders.

But all this makes me wonder how we judge and remember places. I grew up in Princeton, New Jersey, and I know about some horrific things that occurred there. That doesn't make Princeton unsafe. At what point does a place become terrifying and unlivable? When I returned to the Hudson Valley, one friend asked another, whether she felt safe in a particular Kingston neighborhood. We were having the same conversation as on St. Croix.

I'd been worried about the people with dogs, but what I should be concerned about was the empty beaches I so relished. I felt robbed of a simple joy. How much of this was about being female, a single female, alone? I always thought I was fearless. But for three weeks, I didn't go beach-walking. But I couldn't not. I got back on that horse.

A month after I left island that year, a Wrangler was stolen at gunpoint from a couple while they were driving near Ha' Penny and then found hours later down the road.

*   *   *

I had just returned to St. Croix. It'd been seven months since I last drove down the dirt road to Ha' Penny past Dan the Music Man's goat farm, who infrequently I hear playing saxophone in the distance. The road seemed better than I remembered—with fewer, shallower potholes. No one had dumped their old bathroom into the grass on the side of the road. But the same joyful anticipation mixed with anxiety overcame me.

As I bumped along in my rental car towards the beach, I saw a man ahead, walking with determination towards the beach, with a bag that could have been a tied white kerchief slung over one shoulder. Lithe, able-bodied, straight-backed, without a car or shoes or shirt, and who wasn't a runner or biker or swimmer. A lone male. Should I turn around? I had come this far. Where would I take Dexter for his walk which was three days overdue?

As I parked, and got organized, the man passed us on his way to the beach.

Dexter and I were right behind him. I had Dexter on a short leash.

"Nice dog!" the man said, with a broad smile.

I wanted Dexter to seem ferocious, but he just lunged to stick his nose into a crab hole. The surf was high, so we were forced to walk the same path behind the handsome nomad. The man kept moving and by the time Dexter and I got through the trees and bush, he had settled in the shade under the palm tree, a hundred feet in. I wouldn't have noticed or seen him, but I was looking for him.

"Nice spot you have there," I said.

I engage as a defense mechanism. I am friendly and outgoing and look people in the eye and I have for the most part been left alone. But as a woman, friendliness can be misconstrued, even with men I think are friends. I am fortunate to be tall and athletic, but my hips give me trouble and I'm not sprinting anywhere.

"Yes."

"You live here?"

"Yes. What kind of dog is that?"

"Setter. . . .Are you from here? You don't sound Crucian." He sounded American. A kind of neutral accent.

"I'm from west Africa."

"Really? Where?"

"Senegal."

"I've been there. And The Gambia. And Ghana. You don't sound like you're from Senegal. No French accent. What tribe are you from?" I learned that there are over 36 tribes, and six major ethnic groups in Senegal while working for and traveling there with the Peace Corps.

"Wolof."

I had, without meaning to, triangulated whether he was telling the truth.

"You have no accent! . . . I was in Senegal and went to the island off –"

"Goree Island," he volunteered. Goree Island is a tourist destination, a devastating historic site where Africans were incarcerated before they were sent across the ocean to be enslaved. "You come here every day?" he asked.

"Sometimes," I lied. I almost always came to Ha' Penny.

"Where else do you go?"

"I mix it up." Unease was setting in. I looked at Dexter, who was eager to move on. "I'll catch you on the way back. He needs his walk."

"Okay."

"What's your name?" I asked.

"Abdul."

"Cynthia." Why did I ask him his name? Why did I tell him mine? And how did I have the guts to keep walking?

As I turned to move on, Abdul said, "Watch out for those niggers."

I paused long enough to repeat what he said in my mind but didn't have enough time to think why he would say that, like that.

"I've never had any trouble," I responded.

As I walked, I wondered why he used the N word. Was it a warning, or was he testing me? To separate himself from others? To connect himself to me? Had he sensed my discomfort?

Abdul occupied my thoughts for my entire walk. He was beautiful—such striking, chiseled features— and lucid, but I kept wondering whether he was one of those people who seem normal, can pull it together, but can get mental quickly. A friend who worked both in mental illness and in homelessness acknowledges there is significant overlap.

On our return, Abdul asked again about Dexter.

"He's an English Setter."

"He's beautiful."

"Thanks," I said, turning away, then back. "Hey, Abdul, I was wondering where you get fresh water . . . to drink?"

"From the pond."

"I'll bring water for you next time I come."

"Thank you!"

That afternoon, Henry, my go-to carpenter and mason for years, came by to remove my storm doors and hang the two big screens in my living room with me. Henry

is Crucian but lived in New York for over a decade. We've known each other for several years.

    We chatted and caught up. His wife is chronically ill, and he cares for her with tremendous devotion. His days revolve around her: He arrives at ten o'clock, after helping her in the morning, feeding her, and then leaves work at one to bring her lunch. The prior year she went to the hospital to get her meds adjusted and she ended up in a coma which lasted through much of the pandemic. She came home eventually and recovered somewhat, but requires round-the-clock care. Henry has to hire someone for $17 an hour when he comes to work with me. Her care costs as much as he makes. But it was breaking him. He needed to get out of the house for his own sanity.

    She was a little better this year. Some of her memory returned; she was talking.

    Once, when I asked him if he'd ever retire, he looked into the distance and said, "Black man die when he stop working." But we both commented this year, at over sixty, how there are things we can't do anymore.

As we put up the large screen, working alongside one another, he told me a story about someone he knows from Trinidad who is an expert swimmer and was out on a sailboat with four other guys when the boat capsized. Two guys were in the cabin and saved, two died, and the expert swimmer was never found, which didn't make sense.

I told Henry about Abdul.

Henry said, "You know, they say they let people out of prison in the States and fly them down here with nothing."

"No. No. They can't do that."

But that thought haunted me. Could Abdul be an ex-convict? Did he learn American English on Rikers Island?

I didn't go back to Ha' Penny for days. I took Dexter to Chenay, the Windsor Farm wooded hike, and walked around town. I actively avoided another encounter with Abdul.

A week later, I returned with trepidation and a bottle of water, an offering, just in case.

As I rounded the bend on the beach, the grill was still there, as it always was, but Abdul was gone. I wondered whether someone reported him, and he got scooped up and "housed" or whether he found another place to go and where he would next appear.

*   *   *

As I arrived at the Ha' Penny parking lot another morning, a police car angled toward the water. I pulled up alongside and approached the driver side. A young police officer rolled down her window. Her nametag said Officer Joseph.

"Good morning, Officer Joseph."

"Good day."

"Are you here for any particular reason?" I asked. "Is this about the shooting this morning in Gallow's Bay?"

"Yes. Four ran from the vehicle at Spray's."

"They came here?" I didn't know where Spray's was; did I hear correctly? I'd heard of Sprat, which I thought was out near Frederiksted, the other end of the island. But she wouldn't be here unless it were nearby. "So, they are at large? They might be in there?" I pointed at the bush.

She nodded.

"How would you, all by yourself, handle four guys with guns?"

She shrugged, smiled.

"Do you think it's safe for me to walk?" In some ways I felt safer than on other days because she was there, but, in other ways, not so much.

"You should be okay."

"Will you be here?"

"Yes."

"For how long?"

"Ten, fifteen minutes."

"I'll be, like, 45 minutes. Can you stay?"

"No." She looked sorry.

I considered the beach. Empty today. "Okay thanks, Officer. Please stay as long as you can."

She rolled up the window. I got Dexter, the water bottle and bag from the car.

I kept an eye on the police car as I walked away. We passed the teal hotel, the only building on the beach. We were passing the distant sugar mill when I turned once more. The police car was gone, at about the fifteen-minute mark. My heart sank. Dexter and I walked to the end of the beach, almost a mile from the parking lot. This spot felt even trickier than usual because of the alternative access through the bush, over the rocks. I often turn back before I get to the outcropping if I see someone with a dog off-lead playing in the surf. But we walked all the way, and were making our way back, with a high quotient of ignorant bliss (Dexter) and determined trepidation (me). Dexter dug for crabs, he chased seaweed into the water, floated for a moment, flicked his tongue on the water's surface, and rode a wave out. He shook.

We walked halfway back, passing the makeshift, whimsical beach shack made of offerings from the sea, and the colorful overflowing garbage-can pile. Dexter approached me, asking for water. I cupped my hand and poured water into it from the sweating water bottle. He lapped it up and cough-gagged.

Just as I put away the water and stood up, I saw a figure duck into the bushes near a coconut palm, this side of the hotel. I could tell nothing other than it was human, clothed, grayish. Having walked Ha' Penny dozens if not hundreds of times, I like to believe I have a sense for what is normal behavior and what is not. Sometimes there is a new rendition or experience, but a fully-clothed person moving into the bushes is not normal for a beach, this beach. Could this be one of the guys that ran from the shooting? Or was it just a gardener from the hotel (whom I'd never seen before)?

I reached for my local AT&T phone, which was not my normal phone, but I recently got because it was supposed to have better coverage than my pathetic Verizon phone which only worked on WIFI at my house. I got the AT&T phone for precisely this reason: to call 911.

"Hi. I'm on Ha' Penny. I don't want to be alarmist or get anyone in trouble who isn't doing anything wrong, but I saw Officer Joseph on my way onto the beach, and she said you were looking for the guys who ran from the Gallow's Bay shooting."

"I can barely hear you."

"Sorry. My phone doesn't work unless it's on speaker phone." (I later learned sand in the airpod port rendered it permanently on speaker.) I repeated myself. On speaker phone, the waves seemed loud to both me and the woman on the other end. The waves often trip off the "noise" indicator.

"Again, I don't know if it's a man or woman, just human. Oh, wait. He's coming out of the bushes now and walking back towards the parking area, past the teal-colored hotel there. Pretty sure it's a man."

"What's he wearing?"

"Long pants and long-sleeved shirt. Gray and like a dark green or black? I can't really see. Hard to make out."

I started walking again until he stopped. He turned and looked at me. He was 500 feet away, between the hotel and the parking lot. He stood, looking in my direction.

I stopped, too. Dexter pulled. We stood like that for a full minute or two, maybe five; it seemed a lifetime. I didn't know what I'd do if the man started walking in my direction, but our standoff confirmed to me that he was not a normal beach visitor. He was not exercising, or fishing, or walking or building a sandcastle, or surfing, or stripping to go in the water. Min-

utes passed.

Just as I was contemplating how this might end, a police car arrived in the parking lot behind him. He didn't see it, because he was still looking in my direction. A policeperson walked towards the man, and as they got to about forty feet away, the man started walking in my direction, not running, but walking fast, and then headed into the bush alongside the hotel. The police followed him. The whole thing was very calm and subtle but unnerving.

At that moment I wondered whether he in fact was the landscaper or gardener for the hotel, and I felt badly if that was the case, but why would he walk away from a police-person, and double back? I started walking again. As I approached the bright teal hotel whose color always seemed a little off to me, two police officers emerged from the near side of the hotel. The one in front held some kind of drone-like controls and looked out at the sky over the sea beyond me and refused to make eye contact with me.

I said to him, "The guy went in over there, and the other policeman followed him. He might be right there, coming out around the other side of the building."

The policeman kept looking up at the sky in the opposite direction. It seemed so odd. Maybe he knew something more, or things were under control.

"Can I walk by now?"

He nodded slowly without looking at me. I walked towards my car. A policewoman stood in the shadows. I told her everything I knew; she seemed uninterested.

I hope I wasn't a Karen, that I didn't get someone innocent in trouble, and I hoped they apprehended one of the suspects, without incident. I didn't hear any shots.

A few weeks later, they got one of the four guys, but I couldn't find anything in the paper. Every time I searched for Ha' Penny, I found more assaults from the past, a reminder of its volatile history.

This year, a stocky, youngish man with bad skin stood at the entrance of the beach in the shade when Dexter and I returned from our walk.

"You okay with saying hi?" I asked, as Dexter approached him on the narrow part of the beach, pulling me towards him.

"What kind of dog is that?"

"English Setter. You have dogs?"

"Yeah. I got pit bulls." He sounded Puerto Rican. I started to move away, Dexter egging me on. He said, "You don't have any tattoos."

"No, I don't." Apparently he'd run his eyes on all my available, exposed skin.

"I do tattoos. You should—"

"I don't do tattoos." I walked away.

BEACH MATH/ RULES

Sandy Point has many rules.

The beach is open December to April
only weekends
10 'til 4.
No dogs.
No smoking.
No tent or umbrella poles in the sand
on account of turtle nests/eggs.
15 mph on the gravel/dirt road.
5 around the blind bends.

We like these rules.
It makes Sandy Point difficult/
precious.
(My) weekends are planned
around time at Sandy.

There are other rules, too,
unspoken, unarticulated.
Like:

Don't walk across the greened dunes.
And this:
Beach comers
unwittingly set up/sit down
in a geometry
dictated by spatial comfort/norms.

A, the first party/couple on the beach,
laden with chairs/towels/coolers/noodles
plunks down
at the path's entrance.
They have arrived early
and care.
They are invested in this real estate.

Party B heads right or left,
generally right,
sets up camp a hundred feet away.

C, a pair, a group, a single,
heads the other way,
establishes their turf at a similar distance.

Then:
D camps midway between A & B.
E between A & C.

And so on:
F between A&D
G between A&E.
each halving the distance between
in a geometric progression.

Sometimes a group's size
alters the equation for the same effect.

Those who don't follow the pattern may
jar those who are already situated
like someone who
sits beside you in the movies
when there are plenty of seats elsewhere.

Exceptions:

Those with annoying flapping shade covers
are given wider berth.
Perhaps this is why they erect
such shoddy shade.

A smoker or a loud group
may be buffered.

Once settled,

after about an hour of
staving off direct sun and heat
with noodles and drinks in hand
settlements are abandoned.
Parties step toward /
down the slope
into the sea.

In the water
people with noodles float
in looser congregations
echoing the spacing on the beach.

While in the water,
the absence of a human
even when a chair or towel remains
at the encampment
alters the math.
The next party is more proximate
to an existing chair / towel
or on a zag / a few feet angling.

Beach math / rules add up.
Follow them
and everything will be fine.

THE FREDERIKSTED PIER

The western of the Twin Cities, Frederiksted, was built in the 1700s adjacent a deep port and calm waters to welcome commerce. The small town, built as a grid with Danish architecture, was pummeled by an earthquake and tsunami in 1867, and then destroyed by a labor revolt on Contract Day, October 1, 1878, called Fireburn, led by four women, known as the "Four Queens." It was rebuilt during the Victorian era, which garnered some of the structures ornate trim and elaborate ironwork. It has never fully recovered from natural and historical assaults, and to me, this is part of its charm.

It is said that some people who live out east never get to Frederiksted; and there are those who grew up in Frederiksted who have never ventured 15 miles, or 30 minutes, east to Christiansted. But Frederiksted is well worth a visit, even a stay. I find my way there at least once a week from mid-island.

The first couple times I drove into Frederiksted, I couldn't quite figure it out. It may have been a hot, dusty Sunday or a sleepy weekday in August. Nothing was open. There didn't seem anything to open—few restaurants or stores. It was all shuttered. I have since learned that Frederiksted has rhythms all its own and is most alive during the holidays or when a cruise ship is in, when bands and stands are set up along the waterfront.

One of my favorite restaurants on the island is in Frederiksted. CiBoNe, set in a small courtyard a block from the beach, is locally-owned, and does a wonderful job with the fresh catch of the day. It is gentle and slow-ish, so don't go there if you're in a hurry, famished, or an impatient person. Go there to slow down. Beyond the food and atmosphere, and occasional musical performance, the bathrooms are worth a gander, with sassy words and phrases scrawled all over the walls to entertain while you relieve yourself.

There is a whole other side to Frederiksted, and the numerous dive shops provide a clue. Even when you don't see humans, there is a lot going on under and around the pier, where you will experience a vibrant ecosystem of sponges and reef dwellers. Snorkeling or diving under the Frederiksted pier is one of the most amazing, not-to-be-missed, satisfying things to do on the island. Just because it's easy, it doesn't mean it's not good. Visitors are incredulous. Snorkeling that is a casual walk from your parked car? That costs nothing more than maybe $18 to rent snorkeling gear?

In fact, I encourage my guests to rent a slightly better, newer mask and snorkel than the one I own from one of the several local dive shops just for the convenience of leaving our car key with them while we are under water. Unless someone in your party is not joining you—which seems impossible, given what they will miss—where to leave the car key presents a bit of a conundrum. Friends have a combination lock on their pickup, another clever solution.

We park fifty feet away near the Caribbean Museum Center for the Arts, a cultural and community center also well worth a visit. We undress alongside the car, behind the open car door out of cursory modesty. Although snorkeling under the pier affords some shade, I don a long-sleeved shirt and water shorts over my bathing suit. We smear on reef-safe SPF, the only kind sold on St. Croix by law, on exposed body parts: ears and backs of knees, for example. As we head across the seaside, palm-lined walkway, I nod hello to the unhoused man sitting on the curb and cluck at the darting chickens. With luck, I might find an egg in the crux of a palm tree, like I did once. Really. (Not much of an egg eater, I left it.)

The original pier was built in the early 1900s, destroyed by Hurricane Hugo in 1989, rebuilt and re-opened in 1994 as a cruise pier. A year later, it was hit again by Hurricane Marilyn, and in 2017, by Irma. Rebuilt with the waterfront promenade in the early 2000s, a multi-million-dollar project, it now welcomes Voyager-class cruise ships dozens of times per year. If I'm on the ball, I check the schedule before we head out to Frederiksted since snorkeling is not allowed (nor enticing) when a cruise ship is docked.

I used to enter the water to the right of the pier near the burgundy-colored Fort Frederiksted on the north end of town, which serves as an occasional event space, but have lately been approaching from the left, for no particular reason. We walk down the stairs, and clamber over the boulders to where the water hits them in a spray. I wear and kick off the worst pair of flip-flops I own. I stow them by the wall, out of the way. I pick my way with care to the water so as not to pierce the tender arch of my foot with a sharp stone emanating from a concrete pylon; I might warn my guest of the same in my annoying maternal way. I sit down on a flat rock with a critical decision: should I put the fins on while on shore, and have an awkward entry with the waves lapping? Or lower myself into the water with one hand, and put the fins on while standing in the waves? Either way, it's a graceless moment.

Once in, we spit in, lower and adjust the mask and snorkel, maybe shake the sand out of the fins if it's rubbing. We'll head out over the sandy shallow bit, where we might spot a flounder and turtles in the sea grass, then hug the brown rocks around the bend where the first gems will be spotted in hideouts—an eel or a needlefish or an elegant, color-popping wrasse.

If others have recently emerged from the water, I ask what they saw and where; I hope and know we will see more because we will go all the way to the end of the 1526-foot pier until we reach the enormous barrel sponges, whether my guest wants to or not. I will make them circumnavigate every one of the pillars and point excitedly at every psychedelic, whimsical sponge so they don't miss a thing. I want them to love it as much as me, see it all. We'll float among the schools of angelfish and approach and hang with a green turtle without bullying him; maybe an innocent baby who is less timid will stare into our masks.

I'll be the best snorkel buddy ever as I share everything I come across, pointing urgently and shouting through my snorkel. I delight in spotting a delicate coronet fish with its slender profile. If I am with my daughter, Tess, I will see even more, as she finds a whole new layer of nuance beyond the obvious, like the camouflaged, red-lipped batfish, or behaviors and interactions. She knows which fish are juveniles, rather than another species and how some change or acquire gender over time, called protogynous hermaphroditism, like the parrotfish, who's young look a little like what I would have thought a red snapper might. Females turn to males and become iridescent in blues and greens and reds. They may sexually mature earlier if sexually active adults are experiencing a high mortality rate. The wrasses change color as well, sometimes quickly and temporarily. These are my favorite fish, I think: small pops of color, neat and high-design. One of the more common and exquisite are the creole and clown wrasses. When Tess is not with me, I try to channel her, look for what she might, but I don't do the dive-snorkel thing, as she does, to find a lobster hiding inside a shelf twenty feet below.

There's so much to know, but not knowing, it is still—or maybe even more—a place of wonder and beauty. Who can tire of the array and abundance? I've seen many of the fish before, but they are stunning just the same, and each snorkel I experience something new. A sea horse dangling near the surface made my snorkel-day. An enormous territorial barracuda with its menacing toothy underbite was a little too close for comfort another day and encouraged me to swim elsewhere.

And no matter how many times I've visited the pier, I am fascinated by its rich sponge tapestry of unique color combos—purple, green, and marigold covering the pillars, even more colorful when the sun is out, or under inspection with a light at night. Comical phalluses, mushroom-like shapes, some wear berets or cooks' hats or mops. They fight to be seen, trampling one another in a Dr. Seuss-like world. These colorful pillars beat all the reefs I've snorkeled around the island.

Mahi-mahi, which is commonly and safely eaten on St. Croix, is also known as dolphinfish or dorado. And wahoo, which I associate with bigger, chunky fillets is actually a slender fish in comparison to the blunt-nosed mahi-mahi. Grunts, which are frequently spotted (and heard) in the reefs—the blue-striped varietal are particularly memorable—are also good and safe eating, but they are small, so you don't see them much on restaurant menus.

The blue tang is not only beautiful but along with other pancake-flat surgeonfish performs the important duty of eating destructive algae from the reef. The smaller pot fishes keep reefs healthy, too, through their grazing habits and include a wide variety of styles and looks: the chunky trunkfish, colorful queen triggerfish, the red porgy and French angelfish which comes in either spots or stripes.

Many reef fish are endangered and left alone not only because of their important role in keeping reefs healthy, but because as they do so they can carry a foodborne illness called *ciguatera*. In picking away at the reef they accumulate ciguatoxin, a toxin produced by dinoflagellates, which grow on coral reefs. Larger fish, like the barracuda, amberjack, some grouper, bonito and mackerel, accumulate ciguatoxin at high levels.

I am not good with the fish names, but look them up later and try to sear them into my

feeble memory. Green and moray eels are easy to remember, as they carry a certain amount of emotion for this snorkeler. Sting and eagle rays are always a treat as they billow by. The octopus, of course, is a treasure and while I haven't seen one at the pier, I did spend a half hour with one at Buck Island, watching it change colors and configurations and hangouts. I saw a half dozen squid once out at Cane Bay, a decent snorkeling site. At a minimum, you can socialize with a turtle, or an elegant school of fish not only cloned in look but in behavior, as they move and turn in perfect unison.

Not wanting to miss a thing, we will cover the entire pier and even make our way around some of the other sunken wreckage nearby. But if the water's choppy, we may turn around earlier. We make our way back more efficiently but dawdle if we spot something remarkable.

When we emerge from the water, we compare notes. We are waterlogged, exhausted and sated, maybe a little seasick. Our masks are etched on our foreheads and cheeks. The pier is a triumph. Visiting friends are an excellent excuse to go; but there is no need for excuses. All you need is a snorkel and a buddy.

If we've timed our snorkel perfectly, we will catch the best sunset on the island, watch for the green flash, then head around the corner to CiBoNe for some fresh fish and live music.

POLYSANDORY

I know the sweet smell of Isaac's breath
in the morning when
he rolls over and rolls over
and rolls over and beckons
Come.

But I won't go to him
yet.
I lie down with him
once the clouds lift /
after spending time with Jack.

I can love more than one.

I pause

beneath sturdy sea grape tree shade
seeking relief
then I strip / untie laces / peel socks.
I stand before /
reveal myself to Jack.
I walk with care to the water's edge.
I am happy / naked here.

Alone / not alone.

Pelicans drop from the sky / others
chase foam /
hermit crabs roll over too.

Jack urges me to sing
where no one hears my unsteady voice
witness / savor amazing grace
not mine.

When I shake my sandy socks
consider sticky feet / walking barefoot
I am tempted

when he says,
Don't go, stay.
Please.
Stay.

My first time with Isaac was
the breath of laughter.
Rare / seduction / surrender.
You know,
where-have-you-been-all-my-life? kind of
stuff.

I came around the bend on the desert trail
gaze lifting from ground to
inhaling jaw-dropping vistas, pale coves,
the hips of distant ridges,
a welcoming / welcome expanse
of grass and sky, formidable / personal.
I rose early to get there
before the sun was high.
The long drive / calf-cactus scratch
were worth all / forgotten.
I fell hard.
Compelled by intense yearning,
I visited Isaac
every chance.

But he has another side:
brutal / willful.
He made promises he couldn't
keep / keep me safe.

I smelled before I spotted
a bloated deer
legs splayed
hooves in air
just out of the surf's reach.

I let a week between us.

A biker

bumped down / around a blind curve.
I screamed in fright.
I screamed at him.
He called me *tender*.

This is the way
Isaac said. I was unsure.
I had never done / gone that way before.
Isaac took my hand
led me down a fork-tongued path
He let go as I
slipped / gasped / stumbled
on a crumbling cliff.
In retreat
I took the other tong / tongue
lost myself in a sinister forest of
10-foot prickly pipe organ cactus
each hosting / guarded by an
arachnid the size of my pineal eye
8 unequal legs spread in ripped webs / beds.
I could make out

the trail I wanted
not far / impossibly distant.
I could make out Isaac's laughter.

Isaac implored me
move with / find calm / grace.

Now I see him when I can
Saturday mornings,
early / alone / not alone
sometimes Sundays.

I share, too.
When Jack and Isaac charm my friends
I experience rapture
anew.

I can love more than two.

When I first met Ha' Penny,
I was struck by his confidence /
broad shoulders / silent demeanor.
I know how he looks in harsh daylight

and how his features
soften with the afternoon hour.
Generous/greedy
careless/clean
Ha' Penny offers
lumpy rounded surf-tossed log benches/
teal nets sand-laden
with corals mostly fan/
plastic bottles/orange buoys

and re-seizes.

He breathes/eats verse.
He tickles.
Fickle
he pulls away
just when I want him.
I know what it is to be caught
in his unpredictable moods.
I crouched under a makeshift/sea garbage
tent/tarp
waiting for his rage to pass.
I should have known.
I saw it coming.

I heard Pelican Cove was easy.
I wasn't looking for serious/commitment.
At the end of a long day
I swung by,
found Pelican Cove hard to find/
a tease. But we connected and
I developed an affection for
late afternoon shade/
shallow waters/deep crimson surf/
contortionist palms/
reef artifacts/
sea urchin tidal pools.

Over time tides turned.
Palms' narrow shoreline surfaced
a vicious canine

crazy shouting/whispering men
odd entrails washed up on its shores.

Easy/uneasy.

Pelican Cove's winds can be
pushy, relentless/
the sun of Sandy Point without forgiveness.
I spend just an hour on Sundays with Sandy
that's all I can take.

I met Sandy, the greatest flirt of all, late.
Distant/moonish/edge-of-earth-like
impossibly stunning/intense/desired
by many.

And now, sweet Sandy is
not available—his words—
shut down
not available what with
nesting turtles.

I can love more.

Rainbow and Cane binge weekends
jamming-packed with loud music/hot-rod pick-
ups/acres of bare skin and tattoos
an amalgam of locals/tourists/
temporary workers
volleyball/jet-skis/fireworks/

gunshots at dusk.

Weekdays, I drop by Cane and know
he'll make time/space for me.
I sit on/run my hands through
his sand/watch the sun set with/on him.
I have his ear. He has my back.
We are not exclusive
and yet
my relationships are not casual.

I am not the jealous type.
But knowing their infinite seductions
foot fetishes
toe licking
leg kissing
waist lapping
the salty tingle
I am surprised how much I have them
to myself.

I find out why.

They are not always kind:
woman burned with her children in her car
jeep stolen at gunpoint from couple
assaults/robberies

Friends say,
don't go alone.

Alone/not alone.

I start to catalog encounters/
situations
anonymous/my own.
I tread with more care and/too
more determination.

I will not allow fear in/to win.
I will love freely.
But it is not/will never be
the same.

The waves slap.

That won't happen to me.
That won't happen to me.
That won't happen to me.

I lose/gain
my innocence in the sand.

INDEX OF LIFE ON ST CROIX

Things you know/learn about
the southern saint:
42.5 miles south of the others
the distant third/
but clear winner/first choice
28 miles long, 8 miles thick
bracketed by Twin Cities:
Frederiksted/Christiansted
where you just living/
playing tennis/golf/music/on the beach/
eating/drinking
limin'
worried about how cold the pool is.

You know these in/famous folks:
Hamilton
LeBeet
Hugo, Maria
Fritz
Johnny Cake
Jack Spaniard
Jack and Isaacs
The Contessa in that Castle
Ham and his Bluff
SAH-ra(jane)
Win
Honey Man
Wallace Williams
Positive

You know Chaney is not a politician.

You meet/are snowbirds or Crucians
local/committed retirees
West Indians/Afro-Caribbeans/ Palestinians
Other-islanders: Dominicans, Domin-ee-cans,
Puerto Ricans, St. Kitts & Nevisans,
Antiguans, Jamaicans, Trinidadians
and non/fewer/living:
Tainos/Caribs/Arawaks
Danes, Knights of Malta, Dutch, Spaniards,
English, French, Americans, Germans
Nixon/Agnew
Biden after Christmas
Pence, once
Jimmy & Rosalyn at the Comanche
New Yorkers and
many Minnesotans.

There are 150 churches
41,004 people per last/2020 census
168 realtors
FEMA workers who never left
and a lot of lawyers.

You say:
Good Mahnin or *Morning Morning*
Good Afternoon
Good Night/not evening after 5.

You experience
the other-worldliness
of Buck Island's Turtle Beach
precious Sandy Point
elusive tidal pools
the view from Goat Hill.

You know
Hovensa/Lime Tree/the refinery
its history/politics/ownership/environmental
justice/disaster
pros/cons.
You drive by slowly
to see for yourself.

You rake your hand through
Salt Water Bay and stir/light up

bioluminescent dinoflagellates
on a moonless night
and wonder if it hurts maybe kills those
fairy-dust makers.

You see horses in the field /
near the public pool / roadside /
on the beach.
You might ride one.
You hear about underground horse racing
and a casino / track being built
by the airport.
You hope things will be better for the horses
and the young men who own them.
You're not sure St Croix
needs another casino, what with the
one in town and Divi.

You bleat when you see
goats on the hills / in fields / in roadways
not / behind fences
not on Goat Hill.

You get to know
the reefs and their enormous brain/s
corals and colorful sponges
and all those (empty) beaches with public access
the national parks and preserves,
the good works of The Nature Conservancy,
the pacing / counting of turtle empathizers.
You have a favorite outdoor room
at the St. George Botanical Garden,
lament the demise of Whim Plantation
attend openings and concerts / throw pots at the
Caribbean Museum Center of the Arts,
support feral cats, Ruff Start,
Women's Coalition, the Caribbean Theater,
World Ocean School.
You bid on auction items and
maybe serve on a board.

You know
to be on call/watch for
hurricane formation over the Atlantic
after June
and weigh Saharan Dust against
the destruction wrought by a named storm.
You hear the stories about Hugo:
how not a leaf was left on the trees
not a blade of grass
about how those who survived bonded
as they spent the night wrapped in rugs
under their dining room tables
as the island was wrapped by Hugo's wrath.

You know/know why
people carry sticks when they walk
or run through neighborhoods.

You dance to Schindiglers
at The Landing
on Wednesdays after a snorkel.
You dance in the grass
or dance at the gas
station, Ziggy's, every other Monday.
You dance at Bungalows/Cheeseburgers/
Disco Bingo at Deep End
Thursday nights
and Sylvie's Place in the dark with the locals.

You see the Frangipani's nakedness and
brilliant rasta caterpillar dressed to the nines.

You swerve to avoid slinky mongooses
darting/retracing their steps on the road.
You see iguanas running at top speeds

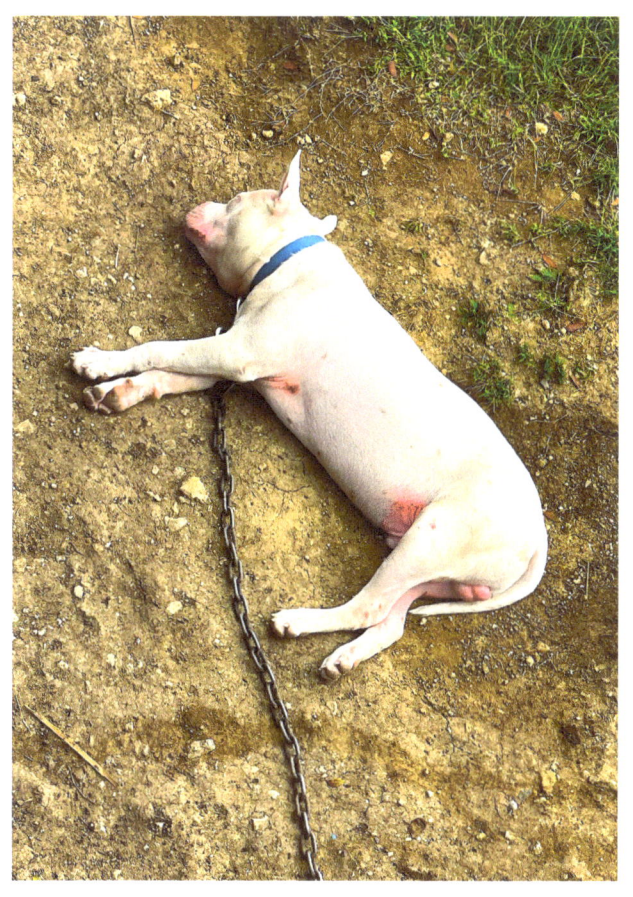

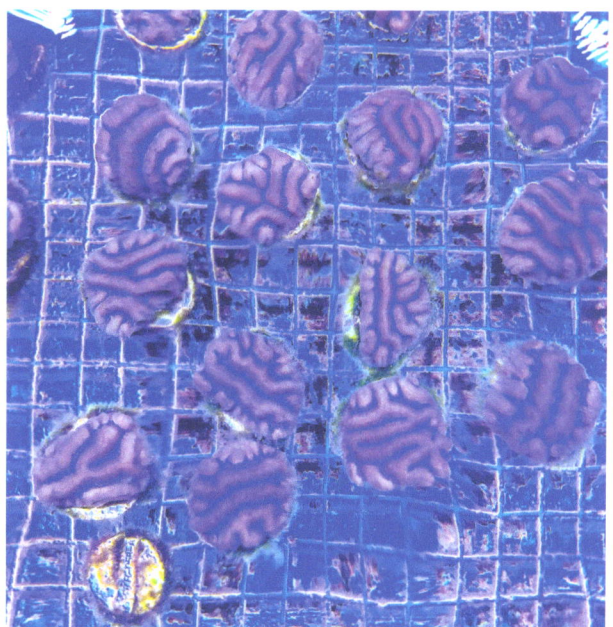

on the beach
by mostly naked phone-scrolling tourists.

Did you know / now you know that
the turpentine is called
the *tourist tree* because of its red peeling
bark?

You eat the lobster roll at Savant
as many times as you can or the
grilled wahoo on a bed of mashed potatoes
at CiBoNe, slowly,
the shrimp with grits at AMA
seated on the grotto at sunset
and, of course,
the rotisserie chicken
at La Reine Chicken Shack.

You go back to La Reine
for the Coquito Festival
and try every flavor at every table.
Stick around for the Ag Fair and try
the goat from the stand with the longest line.
Go to Jump Ups and have a roti
and tamarind sorbet
and look up at / dance with
the Moko Jumbies as tall as the
rakish electric poles.
Pick the right night for the
Christmas Festival or it will be just loud,
maybe when
Ten Sleepless Nights rolls in
or when serious young people play the
steel drums / pans.

Go at least once to the Adult Parade,
maybe for the Caribbean Dancers
in St Croix plaid
but also, for the skin & feathers / thongs /
gyrating / general debauchery.
Put cotton in your ears or you will go deaf
when the speaker trucks "pause" for thirty
minutes in front of you.
Also the tree lighting,
the Children / St Patty's parades.
Go to the Boat Parade every year.
That is fun.

You see rusty Senepol cattle
off Mahogany Road
and come to recognize tan-tan / acacia /
sea grape / flamboyant /
yucca / century plant / ginger Thomas.
You appreciate and comment on the
Christmas winds.

You travel the Bypass,
stop and photograph
the Christiansted harbor
at sunset / sunrise / high noon.
You may contemplate at that moment
that island life is a bypass.

You travel on the left side
on roads that bend 90 degrees
3, 4 times
but keep going *straight*.
You stop to let other drivers in
even when it makes no sense
and others do the same for you.
You toot your horn in thanks.
You come to know the potholes
like unruly children.
You completely stop
when another car comes at you at night
with blinding headlights
and let them pass / by.

By / pass.

If you live here
you will be well-versed in

water catchment and Rooftops,
and HH for your tires and
dead battery when you arrive
for the season and
Poolworks for your pool.
You compare the size of your cisterns
with friends and neighbors
in a not quite competitive way.

You know maybe have an
Island Dog
or bring one back
to the States for adoption
and maybe
adopt it yourself.
You visit the forts in
both the Twin Cities.
Christiansted's little grid
of history will become
your stomping ground/
an old friend/a kind aunt.
You speak about Chris Pardo
as if you know him.
The boardwalk and mill
and always-hungry tarpon
are the embarrassing uncle
who comes for the holidays.

You feast on avocados, mangoes, bananas,
coconuts, bread fruit, fish tacos, mahi
sandwiches, sweet potato fries,
and learn that *figs* are bananas.
You guzzle an island pour of
Cruzan rum, Mutiny vodka or
Leatherback beer and
stock up on frozen sorrel, ginger beer
and green drinks in small water bottles.
You love and recommend but
may never learn
to make bush tea.

You know who has the
best toasted coconut oil
at the farmer's market
and that pistachio cake
can't be *that* green naturally.
You get used to seeing plants by the acre
that are potted house plants back home
and marvel at how West Indians
create an oasis and sustenance from *the bush*/
from a a handful of trees/wandering chickens
in their yards.

You go to outdoor movie night with friends
or are taken for a ride into the
rainforest, see the beer-drinking pigs
who are having a dry year
on the way to the Lawaetz Museum which
may or may not be open,
attend a slow-down dinner
at Ridge to Reef Farm
or hunt boa constrictors in Creque Dam.

You hear about the Fountain Valley massacre/
Carambola/Rockefeller
and know/wonder if/hope things
have changed.
You follow Facebook groups and find
they have/not
and there's a lot of anger/
and some hope.

You learn there is no planning on St. Croix.

You may adopt island time
or, like most,
arrive before the hour
and bring your own chair.

ACKNOWLEDGEMENTS

APPRECIATION

Thank you to all those who inspired this writing: the wrasses and dinoflagellates who light up the water, the flamboyant and turpentines and mahoganies reaching for the heavens, the blues of the beach seas and the brilliant smiles and kindness of St. Croix's many peoples, including those who inhabited the island before Columbus arrived: Igneri, Taíno (or Arawak), and Carib. I appreciate the ears and guidance of my fellow writers of St. Croix's Writers Circle, with whom I've spent many Monday mornings and much of this tome. Jan and Dee Henle were instrumental in sharing the life and artistry of Atti with me and giving me an introduction to the island. Lisa Cantrell, who grew up on St. Croix, and is a neighbor in the Hudson Valley, provided a close reading and offered additional insights and edits. My college classmate, Tim Young, is a generous font of history and story. Thank you, Honey Man (aka Roniel Allembert) for allowing me to share photos of radiant you taking care of my bees. The photographs of Dexter eating the coconut on the beach were taken by my daughter Tess Krasne. Thank you, too, to Bill Stafford for the permission to use the photograph he took of me at Ham's Bluff Lighthouse which appears on the back cover.

PREVIOUSLY PUBLISHED

- "The Resurrection" is excerpted from *Dwell* online, "Flamboyant Hill: A Skeletal Wreck in the USVI with Iconic Stone Walls and Midcentury Lines is Artfully Coaxed Back to Life," https://www.dwell.com/home/flamboyant-hill-7f1b76b3

- "Fresh Impressions," "Houses of St. Croix" and "Blues and Blues and Blues" appeared in *The Caribbean Writer*, Volume 38, 2024

- "Neighborhood Laundry" (as "The Laundromat") "Print Out, " and "Polysandory" appeared in *Mondays at Ten,* November 2020

Written, photographed and designed by Cynthia McVay
Copyright @ 2025 Cynthia McVay

www.cynthiamcvay.com
IG@cynthiamcvay

Some names have been changed.

All rights reserved.
Published by Living in a Place Press.

No part of this book may be reproduced, stored in a retrieval system, or transmitted in any form or by any means, including electronic, mechanical, photocopying or microfilming, recording, or otherwise without written permission from the publisher and author.

There is no permission granted in any circumstance without the written consent of the publisher and author to use any material in the book for AI purposes including training.

Second Edition
ISBN: 979-8-9918639-4-0

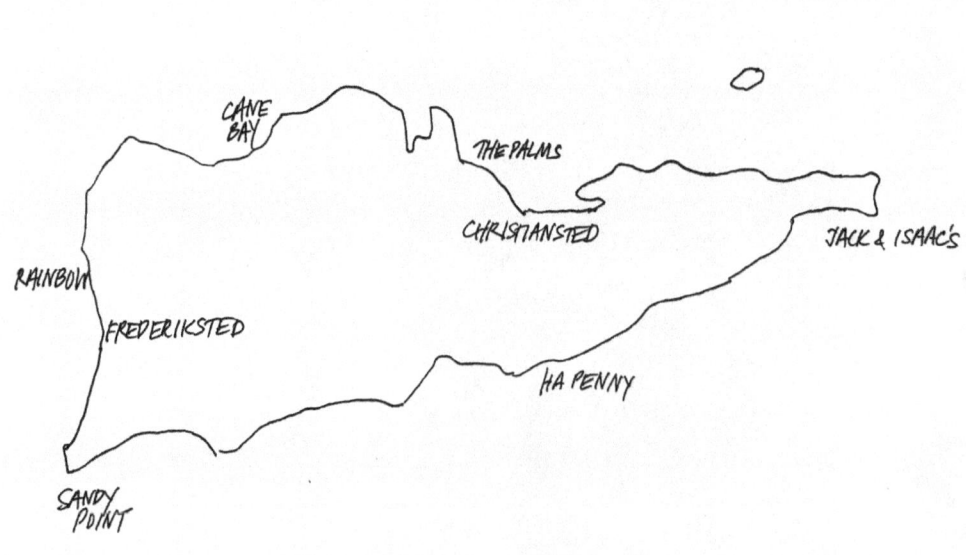

www.ingramcontent.com/pod-product-compliance
Lightning Source LLC
Chambersburg PA
CBHW040903020526
44114CB00037B/48